CLASSROOM DATA TRACKING

Data-Tracking Tools at Your Fingertips!

Kindergarten

Carson-Dellosa Publishing, LLC
PO Box 35665
Greensboro, NC 27425 USA
carsondellosa.com

978-1-4838-3438-2
01-158161151

Table of Contents

What Is Classroom Data Tracking?

Being able to prove student growth is more important than ever, making classroom data tracking essential in today's classroom. Data tracking is capturing student learning through both formative and summative assessments and displaying the results. Further assessment of the results can then become an active part of teaching, planning, and remediation. Because teachers are accountable to families and administrators, and time is always at a premium in the classroom, using a simple yet comprehensive data-tracking system is a must.

This book will help make this important data-collection task manageable. The data-tracking tools—charts, rubrics, logs, checklists, inventories, etc.—are easy to use and modifiable to fit any classroom. The tools will help you collect quantitative and qualitative information on each student's level of mastery in any part of your curriculum. Having specific details at your fingertips will aid in setting goals with students, keeping families informed, updating administrators, and displaying progress at student conferences.

An important component of good classroom data tracking is involving students in their own progress so that they can take ownership of their learning. Statistics prove that when students monitor their own learning and track their own growth, they are more highly motivated and perform better. In addition, a good data-tracking system presents avenues for celebrating student successes. Such opportunities are presented here, whether with an "I've done it!" check box or a rating score, and serve to create the intrinsic motivation we all want to see in students.

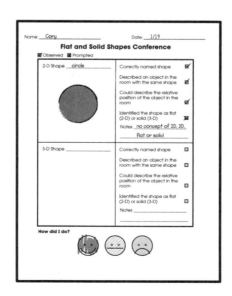
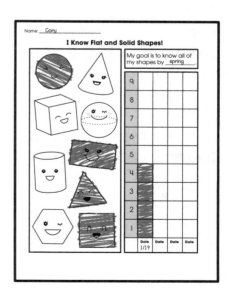

Completed data-tracking sheets for identifying flat and solid shapes

Why Should I Use Data Tracking?

Teachers are busy and do not need new tasks, but data tracking is a must because in today's data-driven classroom, information is crucial. Fortunately, classroom data tracking can be an at-your-disposal, invaluable tool in many ways:

- Data tracking creates a growth mindset. It shifts focus from a pass/fail mentality to one of showing growth over time.
- It allows you to see any gaps in concepts that need reteaching so that you can easily create focused remediation groups.
- It allows for more targeted lesson planning for the upcoming weeks. Pre-assessments can help you justify spending little to no time on skills that students have already mastered or more time on skills where students lack the expected baseline knowledge. Post-assessments can also help you determine whether students need more time or, if not, what topics you should address next.
- It provides you with daily information and allows you to give students feedback and guidance more regularly.
- It involves students with tracking their own data so that they can easily see their own progress.
- It gives students a sense of pride and ownership over their learning.
- It helps create data portfolios that are useful tools for families, administrators, and student conferences.

Data Tracking in Your Classroom

As standards become more rigorous, data tracking is becoming a necessary part of an already full daily classroom routine. The pages in this book are intended as tools that will help you manage your classroom data and create a customized system to make data tracking more manageable. This book is designed to allow you to choose the reproducibles that work specifically for you and your students. You may even choose to use some reproducibles only for certain groups of students instead of the entire class. This book also allows you to integrate assessments into your current routines by using informal observations and other formative assessments instead of interrupting the flow with traditional tests. If possible, try to involve students in tracking their own data by using reproducibles, graphs, and sample work to create and manage their own portfolios (for more detailed data-tracking management tips, see Managing Data Tracking on pages 8–9).

How to Use This Book

This book includes four main types of pages. Refer to the following sample pages and descriptions to help you get the most out of this resource.

Each anchor and domain section begins with a learning crosswalk. Use the crosswalk to help you better understand what students should know from the previous year and what they will need to know for the next year to better guide your plans for teaching, assessment, and remediation.

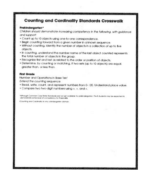

- -

A concepts checklist follows the crosswalk for each anchor and domain. Use the checklist to track which concepts you have taught and when. Write the standard code (such as OA.A.1) in the top-left box and describe the concept in the large space. Use some or all of the boxes to the right to list the dates that you taught, tested, and retaught the concept. Make multiple copies as needed.

- -

An explanation page precedes each set of three reproducibles. Use this page to learn about the intended use for each reproducible, to find additional suggestions for use, and to see an example of the reproducible in use.

- -

The type of reproducibles included for each concept will vary according to the types of reproducibles that are most useful for assessing that concept. Reproducibles may include whole-class recording sheets, conference sheets, open-ended assessment pages, or pages where students take charge of their own goals and learning. Use the explanation page before each set to better understand how to use each page.

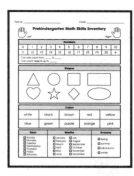

- -

In addition, use the Standards Assessed chart on page 10 to plan for and keep track of the standards and related assessments for a single subject at a glance. Simply record all of the standards for the subject, the dates taught, and any other brief notes you choose to record (assessment types, overall class proficiency, etc.).

Getting Started

You can start data tracking at any point in the school year. If you are new to data tracking, it may be helpful to start small with a single subject until you become more comfortable with the process. Use the following guidelines to help you start a data-tracking system in your classroom (for more detailed data-tracking management tips, see Managing Data Tracking on pages 8–9).

1. Choose the best format for your classroom.
You may choose to have a single binder to collect data or have individual student binders or folders (for more information, see Which Format Is Best? on page 7).

2. Add a cover page.
Because the data-tracking binder will play a starring role in your school year, design an attractive cover that will make the binder identifiable and enjoyable to use. If students are also creating binders or folders, have them add cover pages as well.

3. Organize the binder(s) into sections.
Decide what subjects and topics you will be assessing and use tabs or dividers to clearly divide and label them.

4. Choose a rating system.
Although you may use different systems depending on what and how you will be assessing, use a single rating system for the majority of assessments to create consistency, cohesiveness, and clarity.

Use the following guidelines to help you set a clear tone for the year if using student binders as well.

5. Compose guidelines or a "mission statement."
Guidelines or a short "mission statement" will let students know what is expected of them and make them accountable with their data tracking. If desired, have students keep copies at the beginning of their notebooks and have both students and family members sign them at the beginning of the school year.

6. Have students set long-term and short-term goals.
Long-term goals will give students targets to work toward. Short-term goals will give students attainable checkpoints along the way. It may also be helpful to give students standards checklists in student-friendly language and to have students keep written goals in their binders as reminders.

 © Carson-Dellosa • CD-104916

Other Suggestions

Here are some additional important elements to consider before beginning a data-tracking system:

- *How to recognize students for their successes throughout the year.* Consider ideas such as placing stars programmed with students' names on a Reaching for the Stars bulletin board, giving special rewards, or giving verbal recognition along with a unique class cheer.

- *How to include families in this endeavor.* It can be as simple as sending letters home at the beginning of the year, having student-led conferences using the data binders, or sharing goals with families so that students can work on their goals at home as well.

- *How to maintain student binders.* It may be helpful to provide students with rubrics at the beginning of the year, outlining the expectations for maintaining and assessing their binders periodically to make sure that they continue to include samples and keep the binders neat and organized.

- *How to store student binders.* Decide where to keep the binders—at students' desks or in a separate location. If keeping them in a separate location, you may need to set guidelines for when students can access and add to them.

Which Format Is Best?

Because classroom data-tracking systems need to last for an entire year, many teachers create and maintain them in three-ring binders because of their durability. However, you may choose to keep student work in folders if space is an issue or if students will be storing less information.

A Single Teacher Binder	A Teacher Binder and Student Binders
Pros • Convenient format means the information can always be with you. • You can store all of the information in one place.	**Pros** • Students can move sample work with them each year. • You can include more information because space is not limited. • You have less to do when preparing for conferences.
Cons • You have to gather student work when preparing for conferences. • Space is limited.	**Cons** • It can be time-consuming to work with numerous binders. • It can be challenging to assess class proficiency when sample work is in individual binders.

Managing Data Tracking

Managing the Teacher Binder

- Choose a durable two- or three-inch binder to store all of the important information for the whole year.

- Use the teacher binder as the one place to store the following important assessment-related tools and reproducibles:
  - a copy of the standards at the front of your binder for easy reference
  - copies of the resources and assessment tools for your grade, such as pacing guides, word lists, fluency tests, and reading level charts
  - master copies of assessments (You may also choose to store these separately for space reasons.)

- Consider separating the binder into two sections—overall class proficiency and individual student data. In the class proficiency section, keep information such as what standards you taught when, overall class scores, and student grouping information. Use the individual student section to store running records, baseline tests, remediation forms, and anecdotal notes.

- At the beginning of the school year, assign students numbers and use a set of numbered tabs to organize individual student data in a single place. Add a copy of student names and assigned numbers to the front of the individual data section.

Managing Student Binders

- Consider copying yearlong tracking sheets on card stock instead of copy paper for durability.

- Color code sections to make it easier for students to quickly find the correct pages. For example, copy all sight word pages on yellow paper.

- For younger students, have volunteers preassemble the binders. Include all of the tracking sheets for the year (even if you won't use some until later) to avoid having to add pages later.

- Provide students with several three-hole-punched page protectors for storing sample work, which is often not prepunched.

- Devote a short, designated time each week to allow students to add sample work to and organize their binders.

Tips and Tricks

Organize everything.
- Use file folders to create dividing tabs in a binder. Cut off the half of a file folder with the tab, three-hole punch it, and place it in your binder.
- Keep binders simple by using one pocket for each subject.

Save time.
- Use pens in different colors to make recording dates on a recording sheet simpler. Instead of writing the same date numerous times, simply write the date once in one color and record all of the data from that day using that color. If adding data from another date, repeat with a different color.
- Choose a standard proficiency scale and use it consistently throughout the binder. For example,

E, P, M (emerging, progressing, mastered)	NS, B, OL, A (not seen, beginning, on level, above)
✓-, ✓, ✓+	−, +, ++
a 0–4 rubric	your own unique system

Fit assessment into your day.
- Keep sheets of large labels (such as 2" x 4") on a clipboard. Carry the clipboard throughout the day and use the labels to record any informal observations about individual students. Record each student's name, the date, and your observation on a label. At the end of the day, simply place the label in the corresponding student's section.
- Use your weekly or monthly plan to copy the relevant whole-class progress charts and conference sheets ahead of time. Keep them on a clipboard so that they are at hand when observing students throughout the week or month.
- Focus on assessing or observing only three to five students per day.

Make the reproducibles work for your classroom.
- Add text before copying to create a unique assessment.
- Add, remove, or alter items such as write-on lines or date lines.
- Use a different scale than suggested (see the table above for ideas).
- Use pencil when recording on whole-class checklists so that it is simple to change marks as students progress.
- Use highlighters to draw attention to skills that need remediation, to an individual student's areas of need, or to create targeted small groups.
- Highlight or add stickers beside student goals on graphs and other tracking sheets to give students something visible to work toward.

Standards Assessed

Subject_____ **Quarter** _____

Standard/Topic	Date	Date	Date	Date	Notes

Math Skills Inventories

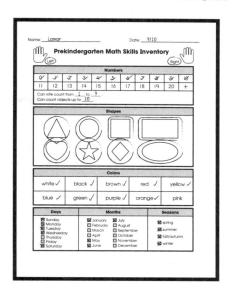

This page can be used to assess a student's basic math skills knowledge at the beginning of kindergarten. This page can also be given to families of students prior to the beginning of kindergarten so that they may assist the child in practicing any unknown or weak concepts before beginning school.

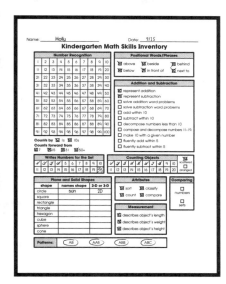

Use this page to obtain a benchmark or as a pretest to assess a student's math skills at the beginning of the year. This sheet can be used throughout the year to monitor progress in math skills areas. It can also be presented as a comprehensive snapshot of a student's progress for parent-teacher conferences. You can present this pre-assessment one topic at a time over a period of days. Use your preferred method of scoring, such as circling or placing check marks over the correct answers.

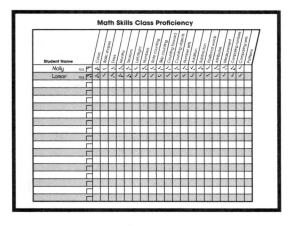

Use this page to keep track of your entire class throughout the year in general math skills. Record student names and the date the skills were assessed in the left-hand column. Use a check mark rating system to record proficiency levels. Present this chart at principal-teacher or grade-level meetings to show your class's proficiency at a glance.

Name: _____   Date: _____

Prekindergarten Math Skills Inventory

 Left   Right

Numbers										
0	1	2	3	4	5	6	7	8	9	10
11	12	13	14	15	16	17	18	19	20	+

Can rote count from _____ to _____ .
Can count objects up to _____ .

Shapes

Colors

white	black	brown	red	yellow
blue	green	purple	orange	pink

Days	Months		Seasons
☐ Sunday	☐ January	☐ July	☐ spring
☐ Monday	☐ February	☐ August	
☐ Tuesday	☐ March	☐ September	☐ summer
☐ Wednesday	☐ April	☐ October	
☐ Thursday	☐ May	☐ November	☐ fall/autumn
☐ Friday	☐ June	☐ December	
☐ Saturday			☐ winter

Name: _____   Date: _____

Kindergarten Math Skills Inventory

Number Recognition

1	2	3	4	5	6	7	8	9	10
11	12	13	14	15	16	17	18	19	20
21	22	23	24	25	26	27	28	29	30
31	32	33	34	35	36	37	38	39	40
41	42	43	44	45	46	47	48	49	50
51	52	53	54	55	56	57	58	59	60
61	62	63	64	65	66	67	68	69	70
71	72	73	74	75	76	77	78	79	80
81	82	83	84	85	86	87	88	89	90
91	92	93	94	95	96	97	98	99	100

Counts by ☐ 1s ☐ 10s
Counts forward from
☐ 7   ☐ 15   ☐ 31   ☐ 50+

Positional Words/Phrases

☐ above   ☐ beside   ☐ behind
☐ below   ☐ in front of   ☐ next to

Addition and Subtraction

☐ represent addition
☐ represent subtraction
☐ solve addition word problems
☐ solve subtraction word problems
☐ add within 10
☐ subtract within 10
☐ decompose numbers less than 10
☐ compose and decompose numbers 11–19
☐ make 10 with a given number
☐ fluently add within 5
☐ fluently subtract within 5

Writes Numbers for the Set

1	2	3	4	5	6	7	8	9	10
11	12	13	14	15	16	17	18	19	20/0

Counting Objects

1	2	3	4	5	6	7	8	9	10
11	12	13	14	15	16	17	18	19	20

☐ scattered
☐ arranged

Plane and Solid Shapes

shape	names shape	2-D or 3-D
circle		
square		
rectangle		
triangle		
hexagon		
cube		
sphere		
cone		

Attributes

☐ sort   ☐ classify
☐ count   ☐ compare

Measurement

☐ describes object's length
☐ describes object's weight
☐ describes object's height

Comparing

☐ numbers

☐ sets

Patterns: AB   AAB   ABB   ABC

© Carson-Dellosa • CD-104916

Math Skills Class Proficiency

Student Name	Colors	Basic shapes	Days	Months	Seasons	Left/Right	Numbers	Rote counting	Skip counting	Counting forward	Counting objects	Number sets	Addition	Subtraction	Positional words	Attributes	Measurement	Comparing numbers	Comparing sets	Patterns

Counting and Cardinality
Standards Crosswalk

Prekindergarten*

Children should demonstrate increasing competency in the following, with guidance and support:

- Count up to 10 objects using one-to-one correspondence.
- Begin counting forward from a given number in a known sequence.
- Without counting, identify the number of objects in a collection of up to five objects.
- In counting, understand that the number name of the last object counted represents the total number of objects in the group.
- Recognize first and last as related to the order or position of objects.
- Determine, by counting or matching, if two sets (of up to 10 objects) are equal to, greater than, or less than each other.

First Grade

Number and Operations in Base Ten[†]

Extend the counting sequence.

- Read, write, count, and represent numbers from 0–120. Understand place value.
- Compare two two-digit numbers using >, =, and <.

*Although Common Core State Standards are not yet available for prekindergarten, Pre-K students may be expected to demonstrate some level of competency for these skills.

†Counting and Cardinality is only a kindergarten domain.

Counting and Cardinality Concepts Checklist

Concept		Dates Taught				

Counting to 100

Use this page to individually assess each student's ability to rote count to 100 by 1s and 10s. In each quarter, or other specified time frame, listen to the student count up to 100 by 1s. Record the last number the student counted up to in the *By 1s* column. Then, repeat the process to assess the student's ability to count by 10s to 100.

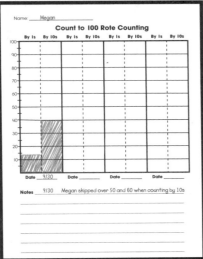

Use this page at home or in the classroom for each student to keep track of her progress. After each assessment, allow the student to color the chart to record her progress in counting to 100 by 1s and 10s. Use the *Notes* section to record helpful information such as specific numbers the student struggled with. Use this sheet as a portfolio tool for parent- or student-teacher conferences.

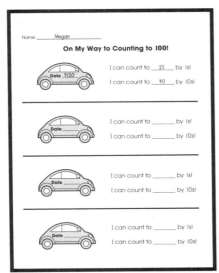

Have students keep this page to record their progress over time as they master rote counting to 100. Each time you assess a student, have him write the date and number he counted to by 1s and 10s.

Rote Counting Class Proficiency

Student Name	Date _____		Date _____		Date _____		Date _____	
	By 1s	By 10s	By 1s	By 10s	By 1s	By 10s	By 1s	By 10s

Name: _____

Rote Counting to 100

By 1s	By 10s	By 1s	By 10s	By 1s	By 10s	By 1s	By 10s
100							
90							
80							
70							
60							
50							
40							
30							
20							
10							

Date _____   Date _____   Date _____   Date _____

Notes _____

_____

_____

_____

_____

_____

Name: _____

On My Way—Counting to 100!

Date _____

I can count to _____ by 1s!

I can count to _____ by 10s!

Date _____

I can count to _____ by 1s!

I can count to _____ by 10s!

Date _____

I can count to _____ by 1s!

I can count to _____ by 10s!

Date _____

I can count to _____ by 1s!

I can count to _____ by 10s!

Number Recognition

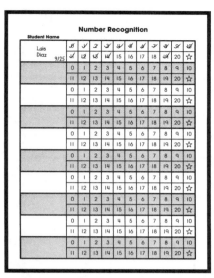

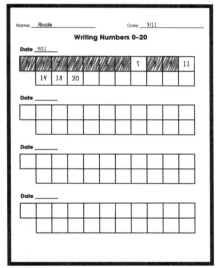

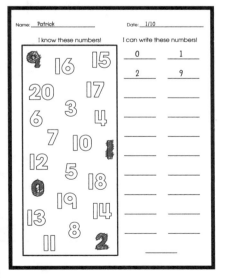

Use this page to individually assess each student's ability to recognize numbers 0–20. Record the date and the student's name in the left-hand column. For each assessment, show the student a number card. Place a check mark over each number that the student correctly recognizes. When all of the numbers can be identified, allow the student to color in the star at the end of the last row.

Use this page to allow students to track their progress over time in writing numbers 0–20. On specified dates, allow students to write as many numbers as they can in the boxes. Then, work with students to color each box where the number is formed correctly and in the correct order.

Have students keep this page to record their progress over time as they master number recognition and writing numbers 0–20. Students should color in the number once they have mastered recognition of it. In the right-hand column, students should write each number they have mastered.

Number Recognition Class Proficiency

Student Name

	0	1	2	3	4	5	6	7	8	9	10
	11	12	13	14	15	16	17	18	19	20	☆
	0	1	2	3	4	5	6	7	8	9	10
	11	12	13	14	15	16	17	18	19	20	☆
	0	1	2	3	4	5	6	7	8	9	10
	11	12	13	14	15	16	17	18	19	20	☆
	0	1	2	3	4	5	6	7	8	9	10
	11	12	13	14	15	16	17	18	19	20	☆
	0	1	2	3	4	5	6	7	8	9	10
	11	12	13	14	15	16	17	18	19	20	☆
	0	1	2	3	4	5	6	7	8	9	10
	11	12	13	14	15	16	17	18	19	20	☆
	0	1	2	3	4	5	6	7	8	9	10
	11	12	13	14	15	16	17	18	19	20	☆
	0	1	2	3	4	5	6	7	8	9	10
	11	12	13	14	15	16	17	18	19	20	☆
	0	1	2	3	4	5	6	7	8	9	10
	11	12	13	14	15	16	17	18	19	20	☆
	0	1	2	3	4	5	6	7	8	9	10
	11	12	13	14	15	16	17	18	19	20	☆

Writing Numbers 0–20

Date _____

Date _____

Date _____

Date _____

Name: _____

I know these numbers!

9 16 15
20 17
3 4
6 10 1
7
12 18
5
0 14
19
13
8
11 2

I can write these numbers!

_____ _____

_____ _____

_____ _____

_____ _____

_____ _____

_____ _____

_____ _____

_____ _____

_____

Numbers and Sets

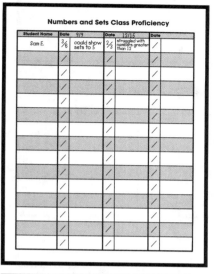

Use this page to record each student's score when assessing numbers and sets. Write student names in the left-hand column. After each assessment, write the date and record the score. Use the blank space to record any notes or concerns you may have about the assessment.

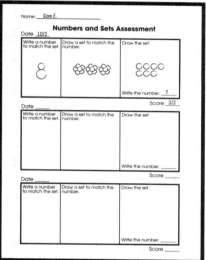

This page is perfect for a quick assessment on numbers and sets. In a small-group or whole-class setting, display a number set. Have each student write the number to match the set shown. Then, say a number aloud. Students should draw a set to match the number. Finally, have students pick up a handful of objects such as paper clips or counters. Students should draw the set and then write the number for the set. Record the student's score below the assessment. Use this page in parent-teacher conferences to show the student's progress in the skill of recognizing numbers and sets.

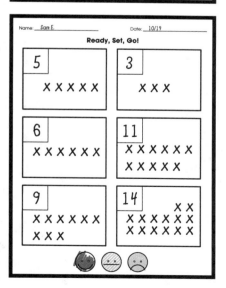

Use this page to assess your students' knowledge of numbers and sets. In a small-group or whole-class setting, say a number aloud. Students should record the number in the upper left-hand corner. Then, students should draw a set to match the number. Finally, have students color a face to rate how they felt about the activity. If desired, insert this page into students' math portfolios to show proof of mastery.

Numbers and Sets Class Proficiency

Student Name	Date		Date		Date	
	/		/		/	
	/		/		/	
	/		/		/	
	/		/		/	
	/		/		/	
	/		/		/	
	/		/		/	
	/		/		/	
	/		/		/	
	/		/		/	
	/		/		/	
	/		/		/	
	/		/		/	
	/		/		/	
	/		/		/	

Numbers and Sets Assessment

Date _____

Write a number to match the set.	Draw a set to match the number.	Draw the set.
		Write the number. _____

Score _____

Date _____

Write a number to match the set.	Draw a set to match the number.	Draw the set.
		Write the number. _____

Score _____

Date _____

Write a number to match the set.	Draw a set to match the number.	Draw the set.
		Write the number. _____

Score _____

Ready, Set, Go!

Comparing Numbers and Sets

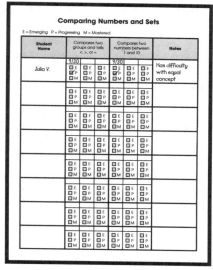

This page is ideal for keeping a record of your entire class's proficiency in comparing numbers and sets. Record student names in the left-hand column. As you present the skills, record the date and mark *E*, *P*, or *M* (note the rating scale at the top of the page) to indicate the progress for each skill. Use the *Notes* section to record dates of mastery or follow-up details. The notes will be invaluable when assigning groups or for conferences with students or parents.

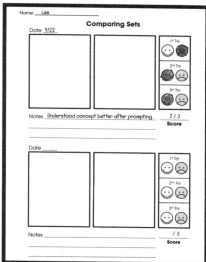

After you've introduced the concept of comparing sets to students, have them complete this page to show what they know in a one-on-one conference. Place a set of manipulatives (or a picture of a set) in each box. Then, have the student tell you which set is greater than, less than, or equal to. Repeat the process two more times. The student should color a face after each problem to indicate how he feels about his progress. Then, record the student's score. Use the *Notes* section to record observations or concerns. This form can also be used as a pretest and posttest if desired.

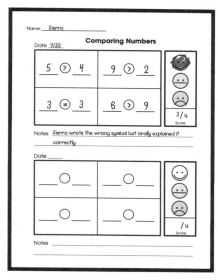

Once students have a working knowledge of comparing single-digit numbers, challenge them to compare numbers to 10. You or the student should fill in the blanks with two 1-digit numbers. Next, have the student fill in the circle with a comparison symbol. Students should be able to explain their reasoning. Record the student's score. Allow the student to color a face to show how she felt about the activity. Record any observations or concerns in the *Notes* section. This form can also be used as a pretest and posttest if desired.

Comparing Numbers and Sets Class Proficiency

E = Emerging   P = Progressing   M = Mastered

Student Name	Compares two groups and tells <, >, or =			Compares two numbers between 1 and 10			Notes
	☐ E ☐ P ☐ M	☐ E ☐ P ☐ M	☐ E ☐ P ☐ M	☐ E ☐ P ☐ M	☐ E ☐ P ☐ M	☐ E ☐ P ☐ M	
	☐ E ☐ P ☐ M	☐ E ☐ P ☐ M	☐ E ☐ P ☐ M	☐ E ☐ P ☐ M	☐ E ☐ P ☐ M	☐ E ☐ P ☐ M	
	☐ E ☐ P ☐ M	☐ E ☐ P ☐ M	☐ E ☐ P ☐ M	☐ E ☐ P ☐ M	☐ E ☐ P ☐ M	☐ E ☐ P ☐ M	
	☐ E ☐ P ☐ M	☐ E ☐ P ☐ M	☐ E ☐ P ☐ M	☐ E ☐ P ☐ M	☐ E ☐ P ☐ M	☐ E ☐ P ☐ M	
	☐ E ☐ P ☐ M	☐ E ☐ P ☐ M	☐ E ☐ P ☐ M	☐ E ☐ P ☐ M	☐ E ☐ P ☐ M	☐ E ☐ P ☐ M	
	☐ E ☐ P ☐ M	☐ E ☐ P ☐ M	☐ E ☐ P ☐ M	☐ E ☐ P ☐ M	☐ E ☐ P ☐ M	☐ E ☐ P ☐ M	
	☐ E ☐ P ☐ M	☐ E ☐ P ☐ M	☐ E ☐ P ☐ M	☐ E ☐ P ☐ M	☐ E ☐ P ☐ M	☐ E ☐ P ☐ M	
	☐ E ☐ P ☐ M	☐ E ☐ P ☐ M	☐ E ☐ P ☐ M	☐ E ☐ P ☐ M	☐ E ☐ P ☐ M	☐ E ☐ P ☐ M	

Name: _____

Comparing Sets

Date _____

1st Try

2nd Try

3rd Try

Notes _____
_____
_____

_____ / 3
Score

Date _____

1st Try

2nd Try

3rd Try

Notes _____
_____
_____

_____ / 3
Score

Name: _____

Comparing Numbers Assessment

Date _____

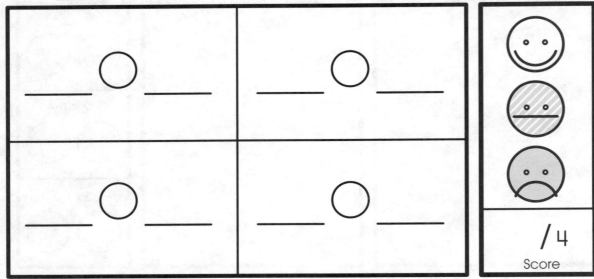

Notes _____
_____

Date _____

Notes _____
_____

Operations and Algebraic Thinking
Standards Crosswalk

Prekindergarten*

Children should demonstrate increasing competency in the following, with guidance and support:

- Recognize that there are more when sets of objects are combined.
- Recognize that there are less when objects are removed.
- Use concrete objects (sums up to 10) to solve practical problems such as, If we have 2 apples and add 2 more, how many apples do we have altogether?

First Grade

Represent and solve problems involving addition and subtraction.

- Use addition and subtraction within 20 to solve word problems with unknowns in all positions (including those represented by a symbol).
- Solve addition word problems with three numbers whose sum is less than or equal to 20.

Understand and apply properties of operations and the relationship between addition and subtraction.

- Apply properties of operations as strategies to add and subtract.
- Understand subtraction as an unknown-addend problem.

Add and subtract within 20.

- Relate counting to addition and subtraction.
- Use strategies to add and subtract within 20.
- Demonstrate fluency with addition and subtraction within 10.

Work with addition and subtraction equations.

- Understand the meaning of the equal sign.
- Determine if addition and subtraction equations are true or false.
- Find the unknown number in addition and subtraction equations.

*Although Common Core State Standards are not yet available for prekindergarten, Pre-K students may be expected to demonstrate some level of competency for these skills.

Operations and Algebraic Thinking Concepts Checklist

Concept		Dates Taught				

Addition and Subtraction

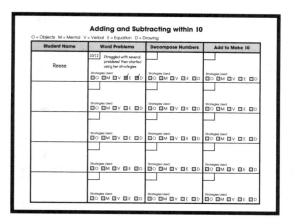

Various strategies are used to teach students addition and subtraction concepts. Use this page to track student mastery of the strategies noted or add another strategy you are teaching. Record student names in the left-hand column. As a problem is introduced, record which strategies you observed the student using while working through the problem. The rest of the box can be used to record dates of mastery or follow-up details. The notes will be invaluable when assigning groups or for conferences with students or parents.

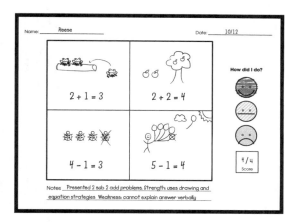

Have students use this page to show you what they know about addition and subtraction. Meet with students one-on-one or in a small group. Present four problems for the student to solve. As the student solves a problem, observe any strategies she used in solving it. Record strengths, weaknesses, strategies, and how the problems were introduced (orally, written, etc.) in the *Notes* section. Allow the student to color a face to show how she felt she did on the assessment. Then, record the student's score.

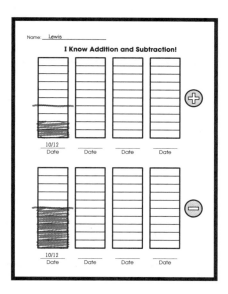

With this page, students can keep track of the progress they have made in learning how to add and subtract within 10. After a student has taken an assessment, have him record the date. He should then draw a line on the blocks to indicate how many problems were on the assessment. To show his score, the student should color a block for each problem he solved correctly. Use the top section for recording addition problems and the bottom section for recording subtraction problems.

Adding and Subtracting within 10 Class Proficiency

O = Objects   M = Mental   V = Verbal   E = Equation   D = Drawing

Student Name	Word Problems	Decompose Numbers	Add to Make 10
	Strategies Used: □O □M □V □E □D	Strategies Used: □O □M □V □E □D	Strategies Used: □O □M □V □E □D
	Strategies Used: □O □M □V □E □D	Strategies Used: □O □M □V □E □D	Strategies Used: □O □M □V □E □D
	Strategies Used: □O □M □V □E □D	Strategies Used: □O □M □V □E □D	Strategies Used: □O □M □V □E □D
	Strategies Used: □O □M □V □E □D	Strategies Used: □O □M □V □E □D	Strategies Used: □O □M □V □E □D
	Strategies Used: □O □M □V □E □D	Strategies Used: □O □M □V □E □D	Strategies Used: □O □M □V □E □D

Name: _____

Date: _____

How did I do?

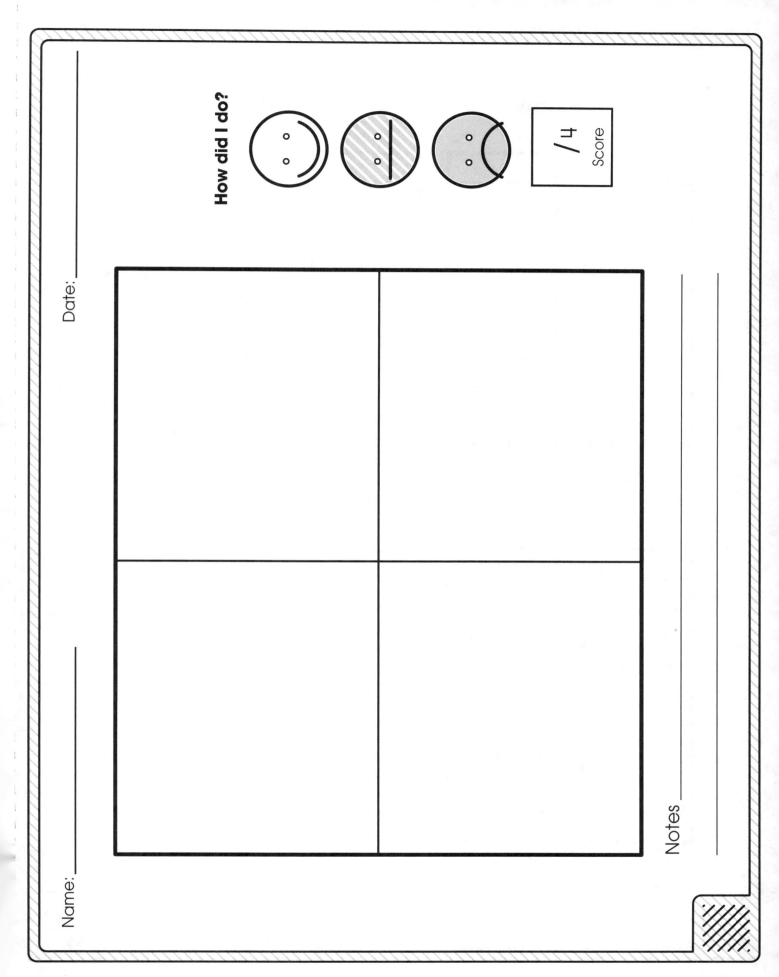

Score /4

Notes _____

I Know Addition and Subtraction!

Date   Date   Date   Date

$+$

Date   Date   Date   Date

$-$

Fact Fluency

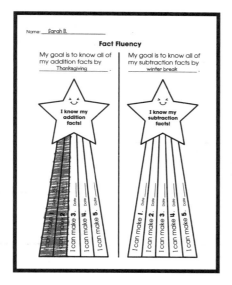

This page shows your class's fact fluency scores at a glance. It can be used for both addition and subtraction. Record student names in the left-hand column. In the two columns to the right, record the date and the score for each fact fluency assessment. The *Notes* column allows you to record observations and strategies used.

Use this page as a fun way for students to track their fact fluency progress. First, each student should set his addition and subtraction fact fluency goals. As students master a set of addition or subtraction facts, have them date and color the appropriate section of the picture. Students should color the star when they have mastered all of their addition and subtraction facts.

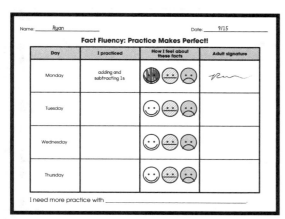

This page is a great way to get family members involved with helping their student learn his addition and subtraction facts. At home, students should record which fluency facts they practiced and how they felt about their progress. The parent, family member, or guardian should then sign the form. At the end of the week, the student should write which fluency facts he still needs help with.

Fact Fluency for _____

Student Name	Date	Score	Notes
		/	
		/	
		/	
		/	
		/	
		/	
		/	
		/	
		/	
		/	
		/	
		/	
		/	
		/	

Fact Fluency

My goal is to know all of my addition facts by

_____ .

My goal is to know all of my subtraction facts by

_____ .

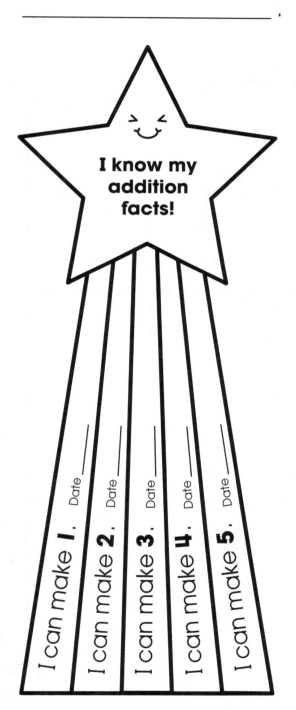

I know my addition facts!

I can make **1.** Date _____
I can make **2.** Date _____
I can make **3.** Date _____
I can make **4.** Date _____
I can make **5.** Date _____

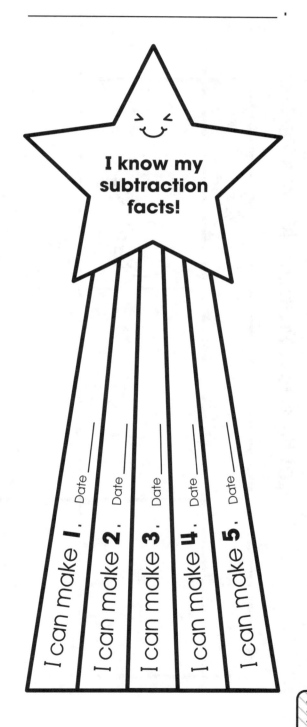

I know my subtraction facts!

I can make **1.** Date _____
I can make **2.** Date _____
I can make **3.** Date _____
I can make **4.** Date _____
I can make **5.** Date _____

Name: _____

Date: _____

Fact Fluency: Practice Makes Perfect!

Day	I practiced	How I feel about these facts	Adult signature
Monday			
Tuesday			
Wednesday			
Thursday			

I need more practice with _____.

Patterning

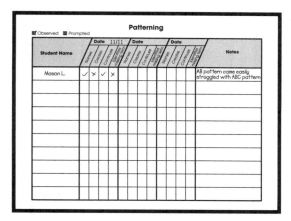

This page is perfect for tracking each student's progress in mastering patterning concepts. Record student names in the left-hand column. In the following columns, enter a level of mastery for each concept (note the scoring marks at the top of the page) and the date assessed. Use the *Notes* section to record any observations or concerns. This sheet allows you to see at a glance which students have mastered these skills and which students need help.

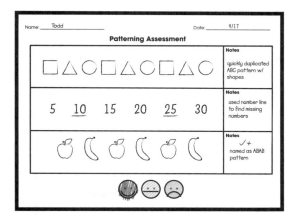

This page allows students to show what they know about patterning. Using pattern blocks, number tiles, pictures, or manipulatives, have the student complete the appropriate pattern for which you are assessing. Use the *Notes* section to record observations about each assessment. Finally, the student should color a face to rate how she felt about the activity. At a later date, repeat the assessment. Keep the assessments in students' math portfolios to show progression of patterning skills.

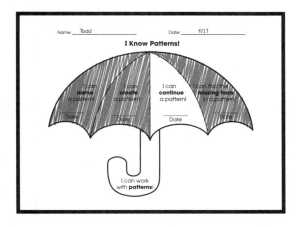

This page allows students to take ownership in tracking their understanding of patterns. Each time a student masters a patterning concept allow him to color the corresponding section of the umbrella and write the date. When all of the umbrella sections have been colored, the student should color the handle of the umbrella.

Patterning Class Proficiency

☑ Observed ☒ Prompted

Student Name	Date				Date				Date				Notes
	Names	Creates	Continues	Identifies missing term	Names	Creates	Continues	Identifies missing term	Names	Creates	Continues	Identifies missing term	

© Carson-Dellosa • CD-104916

Name: _____

Date: _____

Patterning Assessment

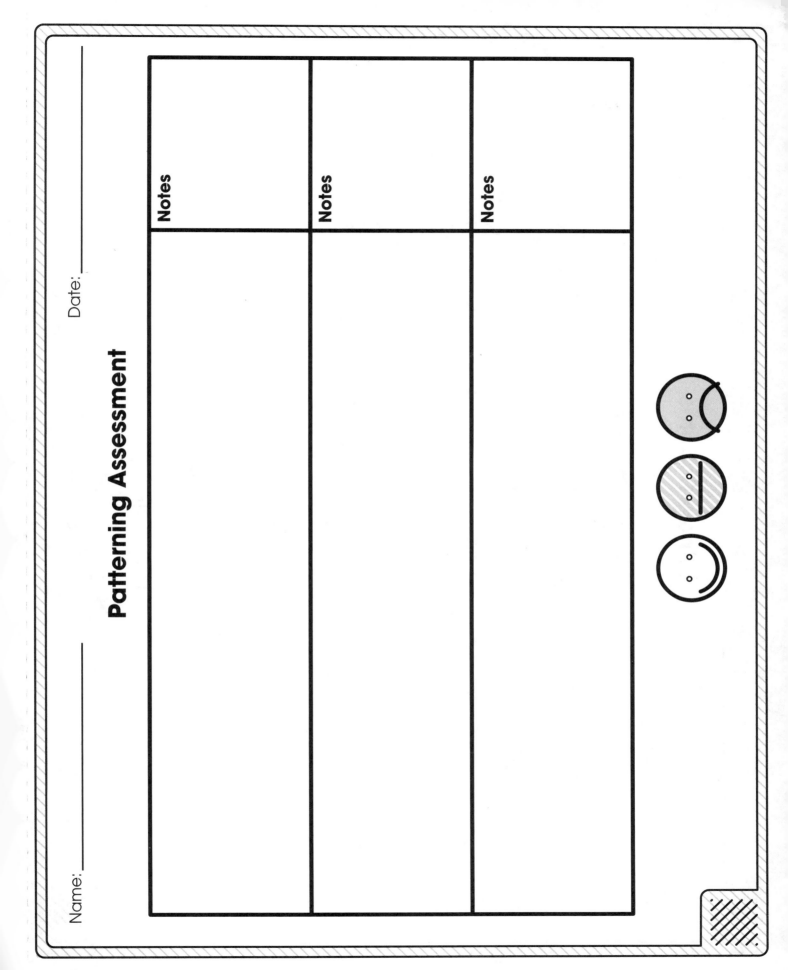

	Notes		Notes		Notes

Name: _____

Date: _____

I Know Patterns!

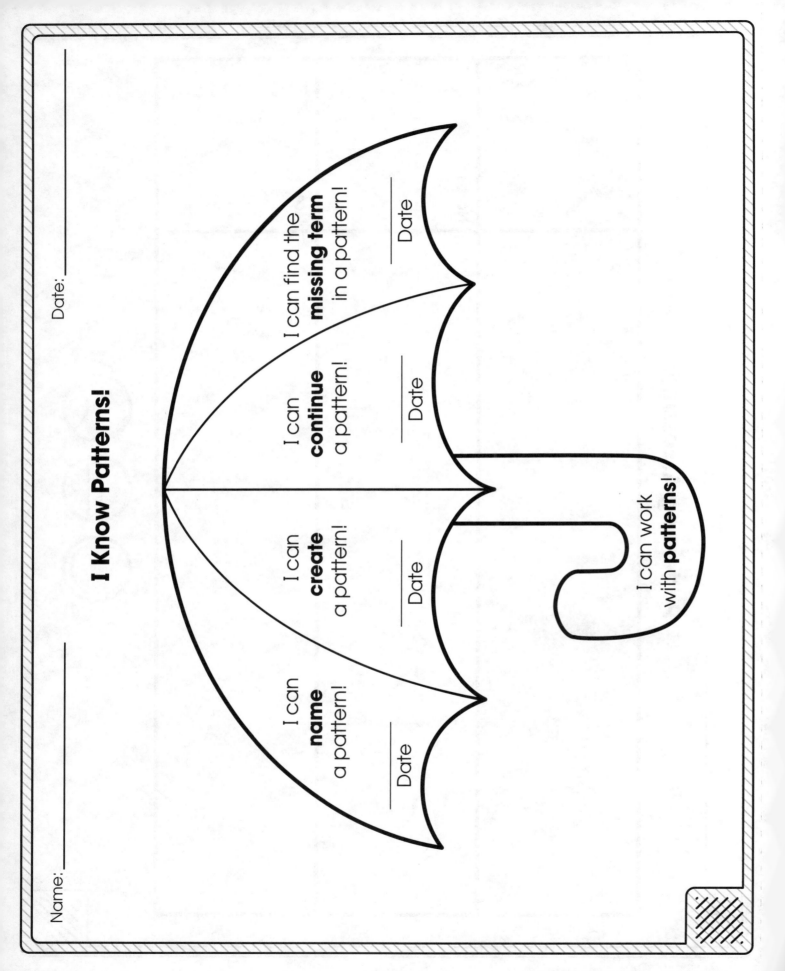

I can find the **missing term** in a pattern!

Date _____

I can **continue** a pattern!

Date _____

I can **create** a pattern!

Date _____

I can **name** a pattern!

Date _____

I can work with **patterns!**

Number and Operations in Base Ten
Standards Crosswalk

Prekindergarten*

Children should demonstrate increasing competency in the following, with guidance and support:

- Recite numbers up to 20.
- Recognize and name numbers 1–10.
- Understand the relationship between numbers and quantities up to 10.
- Combine a concrete set of objects to equal a set no larger than 10.
- Remove a concrete set of objects from a set no larger than 10.

First Grade

Extend the counting sequence.

- Read, write, count, and represent numbers within 120.

Understand place value.

- Understand that the digits of a two-digit number represent tens and ones.
- Understand that the numbers 11–19 are made of a 10 and a set of ones.
- Relate counting by 10s to place value.
- Compare two two-digit numbers using >, =, and < symbols.

Use place value understanding and properties of operations to add and subtract.

- Add within 100, including adding a two-digit and a one-digit number and adding multiples of tens to a two-digit number.
- Understand that in adding two-digit numbers, tens and tens are added, and ones and ones are added.
- Mentally find 10 more or 10 less than a given two-digit number.
- Subtract multiples of 10 in the range 10–90 from multiples of 10 in the same range.

*Although Common Core State Standards are not yet available for prekindergarten, Pre-K students may be expected to demonstrate some level of competency for these skills.

Number and Operations in Base Ten
Concepts Checklist

Concept		Dates Taught			

Place Value

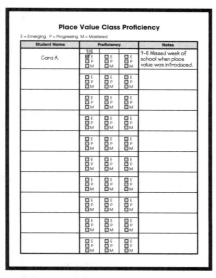

Use this page to keep track of which students have mastered place value with ones and tens for the numbers 11–19 and which students need extra practice. First, record student names in the left-hand column. Take note of students' progress as the unit is introduced, practiced, and concluded by rating their proficiency level (note rating scale at the top of the page) and recording the date of the assessment. With all of your students' progress at a glance, you can plan lessons and assign group work efficiently.

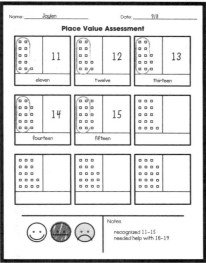

Allow students to show what they know about two-digit place value to 19 with this assessment. First, have the student record the number that is shown in the left-hand section of each block by grouping and circling a set of 10. Then, the student should write the number in the right-hand section and the number word in the bottom section of the block. Finally, have the student color a face to rate how he felt about the activity. Use the *Notes* section to record observations or concerns.

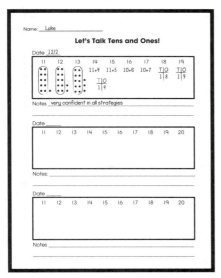

Once students have a working knowledge of two-digit place value to 19, conference with each student one-on-one to have them show you various ways to show each number from 11–19. This page can also be used as a math portfolio piece or as a parent–teacher conference tool.

Place Value Class Proficiency

E = Emerging   P = Progressing   M = Mastered

Student Name	Proficiency			Notes
	☐ E ☐ P ☐ M	☐ E ☐ P ☐ M	☐ E ☐ P ☐ M	
	☐ E ☐ P ☐ M	☐ E ☐ P ☐ M	☐ E ☐ P ☐ M	
	☐ E ☐ P ☐ M	☐ E ☐ P ☐ M	☐ E ☐ P ☐ M	
	☐ E ☐ P ☐ M	☐ E ☐ P ☐ M	☐ E ☐ P ☐ M	
	☐ E ☐ P ☐ M	☐ E ☐ P ☐ M	☐ E ☐ P ☐ M	
	☐ E ☐ P ☐ M	☐ E ☐ P ☐ M	☐ E ☐ P ☐ M	
	☐ E ☐ P ☐ M	☐ E ☐ P ☐ M	☐ E ☐ P ☐ M	
	☐ E ☐ P ☐ M	☐ E ☐ P ☐ M	☐ E ☐ P ☐ M	
	☐ E ☐ P ☐ M	☐ E ☐ P ☐ M	☐ E ☐ P ☐ M	
	☐ E ☐ P ☐ M	☐ E ☐ P ☐ M	☐ E ☐ P ☐ M	

Place Value Assessment

Notes

Name: _____

Let's Talk Tens and Ones!

Date _____

11	12	13	14	15	16	17	18	19

Notes _____

_____

Date _____

11	12	13	14	15	16	17	18	19	20

Notes _____

_____

Date _____

11	12	13	14	15	16	17	18	19	20

Notes _____

_____

Measurement and Data
Standards Crosswalk

Prekindergarten*

Children should demonstrate increasing competency in the following, with guidance and support:

- Compare two objects by length, weight, or height directly by comparing objects side by side or indirectly using a third object.
- Use a unit of nonstandard measurement to measure the length, weight, or height of one or more objects.
- Use measurement vocabulary and comparing terms such as shorter, longer, lightest, and heaviest.
- Classify, sort, and count a number of objects up to 10.
- Sort and classify objects by one or more attributes.
- Work with a teacher to represent sorted objects on a chart or graph.
- Work with a teacher to predict the results of a data collection.

First Grade

Measure lengths indirectly and by iterating length units.

- Compare and order three objects by length.
- Express the length of an object as a whole number of length units.
- Understand that length units must be the same size and have no gaps or overlaps.

Tell and write time.

- Tell and write time in hours and half-hours using analog and digital clocks.

Represent and interpret data.

- Organize, represent, and interpret data with up to three categories.
- Ask and answer questions such as the total number represented, how many in each category, and differences between categories.

*Although Common Core State Standards are not yet available for prekindergarten, Pre-K students may be expected to demonstrate some level of competency for these skills.

Measurement and Data Concepts Checklist

Concept		Dates Taught				

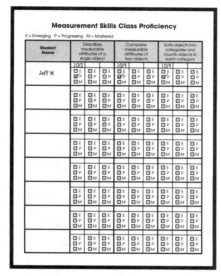

This page is ideal for keeping a record of your entire class's proficiency in measurement skills. Record student names in the left-hand column. As you present the skills, record the date and mark *E, P,* or *M* (note the rating scale at the top of the page) to indicate the progress of each skill. This page can also be used to present measurement skills data at principal-teacher or grade-level meetings.

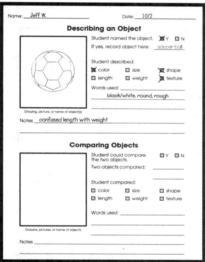

This conferencing page will make it easy for you to note a student's level of progress in describing and comparing objects. In a one-on-one conference or small-group setting, place a drawing, name, or picture of one or more objects in the box. The student should name and describe the object(s). Check the boxes on the page that apply. Record any words the student used to describe the object in the space provided. Use the *Notes* section to record a student's strengths or areas of need.

This assessment page can be used to note a student's level of progress in sorting objects. Give a student a group of objects to be sorted. Write a description of the objects in the space provided. Check the boxes on the page that apply. Copies of this sheet can be attached to a clipboard for ease in taking notes for on-the-spot observations made during classroom work. Use the *Notes* section to record a student's strengths or areas of need.

Measurement Skills Class Proficiency

E = Emerging   P = Progressing   M = Mastered

Student Name	Describes measurable attributes of a single object			Compares measurable attributes of two objects			Sorts objects into categories and counts objects in each category		
	☐ E ☐ P ☐ M	☐ E ☐ P ☐ M	☐ E ☐ P ☐ M	☐ E ☐ P ☐ M	☐ E ☐ P ☐ M	☐ E ☐ P ☐ M	☐ E ☐ P ☐ M	☐ E ☐ P ☐ M	☐ E ☐ P ☐ M
	☐ E ☐ P ☐ M	☐ E ☐ P ☐ M	☐ E ☐ P ☐ M	☐ E ☐ P ☐ M	☐ E ☐ P ☐ M	☐ E ☐ P ☐ M	☐ E ☐ P ☐ M	☐ E ☐ P ☐ M	☐ E ☐ P ☐ M
	☐ E ☐ P ☐ M	☐ E ☐ P ☐ M	☐ E ☐ P ☐ M	☐ E ☐ P ☐ M	☐ E ☐ P ☐ M	☐ E ☐ P ☐ M	☐ E ☐ P ☐ M	☐ E ☐ P ☐ M	☐ E ☐ P ☐ M
	☐ E ☐ P ☐ M	☐ E ☐ P ☐ M	☐ E ☐ P ☐ M	☐ E ☐ P ☐ M	☐ E ☐ P ☐ M	☐ E ☐ P ☐ M	☐ E ☐ P ☐ M	☐ E ☐ P ☐ M	☐ E ☐ P ☐ M
	☐ E ☐ P ☐ M	☐ E ☐ P ☐ M	☐ E ☐ P ☐ M	☐ E ☐ P ☐ M	☐ E ☐ P ☐ M	☐ E ☐ P ☐ M	☐ E ☐ P ☐ M	☐ E ☐ P ☐ M	☐ E ☐ P ☐ M
	☐ E ☐ P ☐ M	☐ E ☐ P ☐ M	☐ E ☐ P ☐ M	☐ E ☐ P ☐ M	☐ E ☐ P ☐ M	☐ E ☐ P ☐ M	☐ E ☐ P ☐ M	☐ E ☐ P ☐ M	☐ E ☐ P ☐ M
	☐ E ☐ P ☐ M	☐ E ☐ P ☐ M	☐ E ☐ P ☐ M	☐ E ☐ P ☐ M	☐ E ☐ P ☐ M	☐ E ☐ P ☐ M	☐ E ☐ P ☐ M	☐ E ☐ P ☐ M	☐ E ☐ P ☐ M
	☐ E ☐ P ☐ M	☐ E ☐ P ☐ M	☐ E ☐ P ☐ M	☐ E ☐ P ☐ M	☐ E ☐ P ☐ M	☐ E ☐ P ☐ M	☐ E ☐ P ☐ M	☐ E ☐ P ☐ M	☐ E ☐ P ☐ M

Name: _____   Date: _____

Describing an Object

[   ]

Drawing, picture, or name of object(s)

Student named the object. ☐ Y ☐ N

If yes, record object here: _____

Student described:

☐ color   ☐ size   ☐ shape

☐ length   ☐ weight   ☐ texture

Words used: _____

_____

_____

Notes _____

_____

Comparing Objects

[   ]

Drawings, pictures, or names of objects

Student could compare   ☐ Y ☐ N
the two objects.

Two objects compared: _____

_____

Student compared:

☐ color   ☐ size   ☐ shape

☐ length   ☐ weight   ☐ texture

Words used: _____

_____

_____

Notes _____

_____

Sorting Objects Assessment

Name _____

Date _____

Description of objects given:

_____

_____

_____

_____

Student counted the objects in each group.

☐ Y ☐ N

Student could sort by count.

☐ Y ☐ N

Notes _____

_____

_____

Name _____

Date _____

Description of objects given:

_____

_____

_____

_____

Student counted the objects in each group.

☐ Y ☐ N

Student could sort by count.

☐ Y ☐ N

Notes _____

_____

_____

Name _____

Date _____

Description of objects given:

_____

_____

_____

_____

Student counted the objects in each group.

☐ Y ☐ N

Student could sort by count.

☐ Y ☐ N

Notes _____

_____

_____

Name _____

Date _____

Description of objects given:

_____

_____

_____

_____

Student counted the objects in each group.

☐ Y ☐ N

Student could sort by count.

☐ Y ☐ N

Notes _____

_____

_____

Calendar Skills

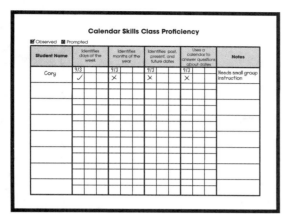

This class proficiency page allows you to see at a glance where students are in their knowledge of calendar skills. Record student names in the left-hand column. In the following columns, enter a level of mastery for each concept (note the scoring marks at the top of the page) and the date assessed. Use the *Notes* section to record any observations or concerns.

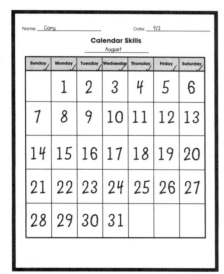

Use this blank calendar to assess your students' knowledge of calendar skills. It can be used in tandem with page 62 to help assess calendar concepts. This page can also be used to teach and assess many calendar concepts such as weekend vs. weekday, days of the week, today (yesterday, tomorrow), and counting.

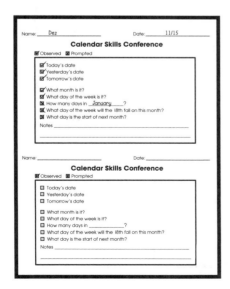

After you've introduced calendar skills, use this page as a guide for one-on-one conferences. Provide a current calendar to the student. Then, conference with him using the questions listed on the conference sheet. Check the boxes on the page that apply (see the scoring marks at the top of the page). Use the *Notes* section to record observations, strengths, and weaknesses. This form can also be used as a pretest and posttest if desired.

Calendar Skills Class Proficiency

✓ Observed ☒ Prompted

Student Name	Identifies days of the week			Identifies months of the year			Identifies past, present, and future dates			Uses a calendar to answer questions about dates			Notes

Name: _____   Date: _____

Calendar Skills

_____

Sunday	Monday	Tuesday	Wednesday	Thursday	Friday	Saturday

Name: _____   Date: _____

Calendar Skills Conference

☑ Observed   ☒ Prompted

☐ Today's date
☐ Yesterday's date
☐ Tomorrow's date

☐ What month is it?
☐ What day of the week is it?
☐ How many days in _____?
☐ What day of the week will the 18th fall on this month?
☐ What day is the start of next month?

Notes _____

_____

Name: _____   Date: _____

Calendar Skills Conference

☑ Observed   ☒ Prompted

☐ Today's date
☐ Yesterday's date
☐ Tomorrow's date

☐ What month is it?
☐ What day of the week is it?
☐ How many days in _____?
☐ What day of the week will the 18th fall on this month?
☐ What day is the start of next month?

Notes _____

_____

Geometry
Standards Crosswalk

Prekindergarten*

Children should demonstrate increasing competency in the following, with guidance and support:

- Identify, describe, and construct different shapes including squares, circles, triangles, rectangles, hexagons, cubes, cones, cylinders, and spheres.
- Describe objects in the environment using names of shapes.
- Use positional words to identify positions of objects and people such as above, below, behind, and under.
- Identify shapes as two-dimensional (flat or plane) or three-dimensional (solid).
- Compose larger shapes from simple shapes.
- Create a picture or design with different shapes.

First Grade

Reason with shapes and their attributes.

- Distinguish between defining attributes and non-defining attributes.
- Build and draw shapes with defining attributes.
- Compose two-dimensional shapes (rectangles, squares, trapezoids, triangles, half circles, and quarter circles) or three-dimensional shapes (cubes, right rectangular prisms, right circular cones, and right circular cylinders) to create a composite shape, and compose new shapes from the composite shape.
- Partition circles and rectangles into two and four equal shares, using the words *halves*, *fourths*, and *quarters* to describe the shares.
- Understand that decomposing a whole into equal shares creates smaller shares.

*Although Common Core State Standards are not yet available for prekindergarten, Pre-K students may be expected to demonstrate some level of competency for these skills.

Geometry Concepts Checklist

Concept		Dates Taught				

Flat and Solid Shapes

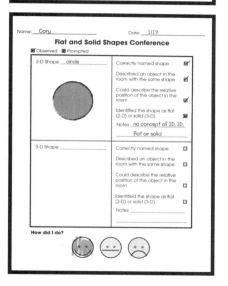

This page is perfect for tracking which students can describe and identify flat and solid shapes. Record student names in the left-hand column. Enter a level of mastery in the following columns. As you present the skills, record the date and mark *E*, *P*, or *M* (note the rating scale at the top of the page) to indicate the level of mastery for each skill. This will allow you to see at a glance which students have mastered these skills and which students need help.

This conferencing page allows you to track a student's ability to identify flat and solid shapes. It can also be used as proof of mastery for a student's portfolio. Present the student with a pattern block shape (or picture of a flat shape) of your choosing. Check the boxes (see the scoring marks at the top of the page) that apply. Then, repeat the process with a solid shape (or picture of a solid shape). Use the *Notes* section to record any strengths, weaknesses, or observations. Finally, have the student color the appropriate face to indicate how he felt he did on the activity.

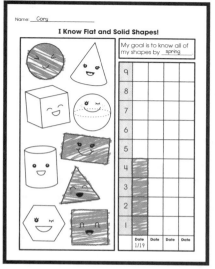

This page is perfect for helping students track their own progress in identifying flat and solid shapes. Begin by having students set a goal at the beginning of the year. As the student masters each shape, allow her to color the shape. The student should fill in the bar graph with the number of shapes she knows for each date assessed. This page is also ideal for use in parent-teacher conferences.

Flat and Solid Shapes Class Proficiency

E = Emerging   P = Progressing   M = Mastered

Student Name	Describes an object in the environment using the correct name and relative position			Correctly names shapes regardless of size or orientation			Identifies shapes as 2-D (flat) or 3-D (solid)		
	☐ E ☐ P ☐ M	☐ E ☐ P ☐ M	☐ E ☐ P ☐ M	☐ E ☐ P ☐ M	☐ E ☐ P ☐ M	☐ E ☐ P ☐ M	☐ E ☐ P ☐ M	☐ E ☐ P ☐ M	☐ E ☐ P ☐ M
	☐ E ☐ P ☐ M	☐ E ☐ P ☐ M	☐ E ☐ P ☐ M	☐ E ☐ P ☐ M	☐ E ☐ P ☐ M	☐ E ☐ P ☐ M	☐ E ☐ P ☐ M	☐ E ☐ P ☐ M	☐ E ☐ P ☐ M
	☐ E ☐ P ☐ M	☐ E ☐ P ☐ M	☐ E ☐ P ☐ M	☐ E ☐ P ☐ M	☐ E ☐ P ☐ M	☐ E ☐ P ☐ M	☐ E ☐ P ☐ M	☐ E ☐ P ☐ M	☐ E ☐ P ☐ M
	☐ E ☐ P ☐ M	☐ E ☐ P ☐ M	☐ E ☐ P ☐ M	☐ E ☐ P ☐ M	☐ E ☐ P ☐ M	☐ E ☐ P ☐ M	☐ E ☐ P ☐ M	☐ E ☐ P ☐ M	☐ E ☐ P ☐ M
	☐ E ☐ P ☐ M	☐ E ☐ P ☐ M	☐ E ☐ P ☐ M	☐ E ☐ P ☐ M	☐ E ☐ P ☐ M	☐ E ☐ P ☐ M	☐ E ☐ P ☐ M	☐ E ☐ P ☐ M	☐ E ☐ P ☐ M
	☐ E ☐ P ☐ M	☐ E ☐ P ☐ M	☐ E ☐ P ☐ M	☐ E ☐ P ☐ M	☐ E ☐ P ☐ M	☐ E ☐ P ☐ M	☐ E ☐ P ☐ M	☐ E ☐ P ☐ M	☐ E ☐ P ☐ M
	☐ E ☐ P ☐ M	☐ E ☐ P ☐ M	☐ E ☐ P ☐ M	☐ E ☐ P ☐ M	☐ E ☐ P ☐ M	☐ E ☐ P ☐ M	☐ E ☐ P ☐ M	☐ E ☐ P ☐ M	☐ E ☐ P ☐ M
	☐ E ☐ P ☐ M	☐ E ☐ P ☐ M	☐ E ☐ P ☐ M	☐ E ☐ P ☐ M	☐ E ☐ P ☐ M	☐ E ☐ P ☐ M	☐ E ☐ P ☐ M	☐ E ☐ P ☐ M	☐ E ☐ P ☐ M

Name: _____   Date: _____

Flat and Solid Shapes Conference

☑ Observed   ☒ Prompted

2-D Shape _____	Correctly named shape ☐
	Described an object in the room with the same shape ☐
	Could describe the relative position of the object in the room ☐
	Identified the shape as flat (2-D) or solid (3-D) ☐
	Notes _____
	_____
3-D Shape _____	Correctly named shape ☐
	Described an object in the room with the same shape ☐
	Could describe the relative position of the object in the room ☐
	Identified the shape as flat (2-D) or solid (3-D) ☐
	Notes _____
	_____

How did I do?

Name: _____

I Know Flat and Solid Shapes!

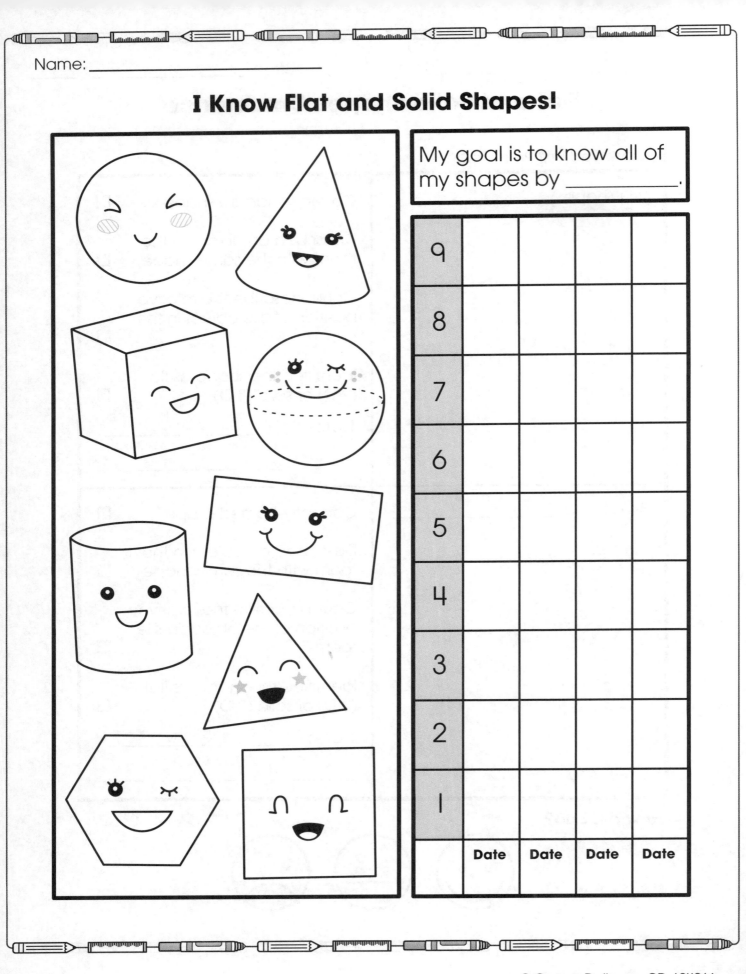

My goal is to know all of my shapes by _____.

	Date	Date	Date	Date
9				
8				
7				
6				
5				
4				
3				
2				
1				

Composing and Creating Shapes

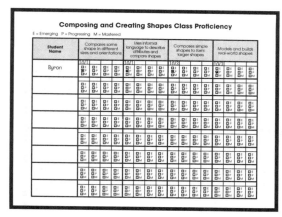

This page is ideal for keeping track of your entire class's proficiency in composing and creating shapes. Record student names in the left-hand column. As you present the skills, record the date and mark *E*, *P*, or *M* (note the rating scale at the top of the page) to indicate the level of mastery for each skill.

This conferencing page will make it easy for you to track a student's progress in analyzing, comparing, and composing shapes. In the top-left box, draw or show two shapes. Check the appropriate boxes on the page as you talk with the student about the shapes. Then, have the student draw the two shapes. In the bottom-left box, allow the student to choose pattern blocks to create and compose another shape. The student should then trace the new shape. Check the appropriate boxes as you observe. Use the *Notes* sections to record any strengths, weaknesses, or observations.

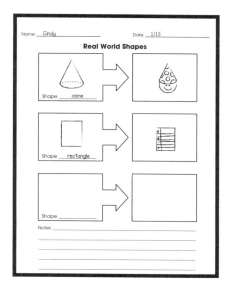

Use this page for students to prove mastery of real-world shapes. You or the student should draw a flat or solid shape in the first box. The student should draw an example of a real-world object of the first shape in the box on the right. Continue with different flat and solid shapes for the next two boxes. Use the *Notes* section to record any observations, strengths, or weaknesses.

Composing and Creating Shapes Class Proficiency

E = Emerging   P = Progressing   M = Mastered

Student Name	Compares same shape in different sizes and orientations				Uses informal language to describe attributes and compare shapes				Composes simple shapes to form larger shapes				Models and builds real-world shapes			
	E P M	E P M	E P M	E P M	E P M	E P M	E P M	E P M	E P M	E P M	E P M	E P M	E P M	E P M	E P M	E P M
	□□□	□□□	□□□	□□□	□□□	□□□	□□□	□□□	□□□	□□□	□□□	□□□	□□□	□□□	□□□	□□□
	□□□	□□□	□□□	□□□	□□□	□□□	□□□	□□□	□□□	□□□	□□□	□□□	□□□	□□□	□□□	□□□
	□□□	□□□	□□□	□□□	□□□	□□□	□□□	□□□	□□□	□□□	□□□	□□□	□□□	□□□	□□□	□□□
	□□□	□□□	□□□	□□□	□□□	□□□	□□□	□□□	□□□	□□□	□□□	□□□	□□□	□□□	□□□	□□□
	□□□	□□□	□□□	□□□	□□□	□□□	□□□	□□□	□□□	□□□	□□□	□□□	□□□	□□□	□□□	□□□
	□□□	□□□	□□□	□□□	□□□	□□□	□□□	□□□	□□□	□□□	□□□	□□□	□□□	□□□	□□□	□□□
	□□□	□□□	□□□	□□□	□□□	□□□	□□□	□□□	□□□	□□□	□□□	□□□	□□□	□□□	□□□	□□□
	□□□	□□□	□□□	□□□	□□□	□□□	□□□	□□□	□□□	□□□	□□□	□□□	□□□	□□□	□□□	□□□

Analyzing, Comparing, and Creating Shapes

Analyze and Compare

Shapes used: _____

Student could name the shapes?
☐ Y   ☐ N

If so, what shapes? _____

Student compared the same shape in different:

☐ sizes   ☐ orientations

Student used informal language to describe similarities, differences, and attributes.
☐ Y   ☐ N

If yes, words used: _____

_____

Notes _____

_____

Compose

Shapes used: _____

Student could name smaller shapes.
☐ Y   ☐ N

Student could form a new, larger shape.
☐ Y   ☐ N

Student could name the new shape.
☐ Y   ☐ N

Notes _____

_____

_____

_____

_____

Name: _____ Date: _____

Real-World Shapes

Shape _____

Shape _____

Shape _____

Notes _____

_____

_____

_____

Language Arts Skills Inventories

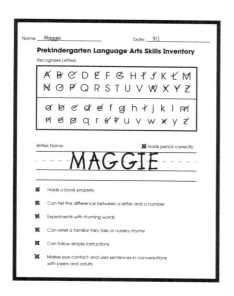

Use this page to assess a student's previous language arts skills knowledge at the beginning of kindergarten. This page can also be given to families of students prior to the beginning of kindergarten so that they may assist the child in practicing any unknown or weak concepts before beginning school.

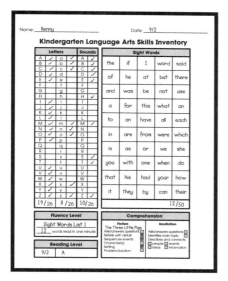

Use this page to obtain a benchmark or as a pretest to assess a student's language arts skills at the beginning of the year. This sheet can be used throughout the year to monitor progress in language arts skills. It can also be presented as a comprehensive snapshot of a student's progress for parent-teacher conferences. You can present the assessment items one topic at a time over a period of days. Use your preferred method of scoring, such as circling or placing check marks over the correct answers.

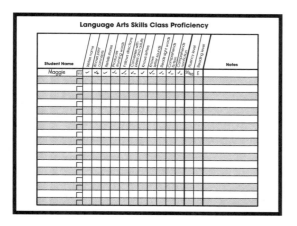

Use this page to keep track of your entire class throughout the year in language arts skills. Record student names and the date the skills were assessed in the left-hand column. Use a check mark rating system to record proficiency levels. Record fluency and reading levels in the correct columns. Use the *Notes* section to record any observations. Present this page at principal-teacher or grade-level meetings to show your class's proficiency at a glance.

Name: _____   Date: _____

Prekindergarten Language Arts Skills Inventory

Recognizes Letters

A B C D E F G H I J K L M
N O P Q R S T U V W X Y Z

a b c d e f g h i j k l m
n o p q r s t u v w x y z

Writes Name   ☐ Holds pencil correctly

_____

- -

_____

_____

☐   Holds a book properly

☐   Can tell the difference between a letter and a number

☐   Experiments with rhyming words

☐   Can retell a familiar fairy tale or nursery rhyme

☐   Can follow simple instructions

☐   Makes eye contact and uses sentences in conversations
    with peers and adults

Name: _____   Date: _____

Kindergarten Language Arts Skills Inventory

Letters				Sounds	
A		a		A	
B		b		B	
C		c		C	
D		d		D	
E		e		E	
F		f		F	
G		g		G	
H		h		H	
I		i		I	
J		j		J	
K		k		K	
L		l		L	
M		m		M	
N		n		N	
O		o		O	
P		p		P	
Q		q		Q	
R		r		R	
S		s		S	
T		t		T	
U		u		U	
V		v		V	
W		w		W	
X		x		X	
Y		y		Y	
Z		z		Z	
/26		/26		/26	

Sight Words

/

Fluency Level

_____

_____ words read in one minute

Reading Level

Comprehension

Fiction	Nonfiction
Asks/answers questions ☐	Asks/answers questions ☐
Retells with detail ☐	Identifies main topic ☐
Sequences events ☐	Describes and connects:
Character(s) ☐	☐ people ☐ events
Setting ☐	☐ ideas ☐ information
Problem/solution ☐	

Language Arts Skills Class Proficiency

Student Name	Writes name	Knows print concepts	Retells stories	Produces rhyming words	Follows directions	Converses with peers and adults	Knows letters	Knows letter sounds	Reads sight words	Comprehends fiction	Comprehends nonfiction	Fluency level	Reading level	Notes

Reading: Literature
Standards Crosswalk

Prekindergarten*

Children should demonstrate increasing competency in the following, with prompting and support:

• Ask and answer questions about a story or poem that is read aloud.
• Retell main ideas from a story or poem that is read aloud.
• Ask and answer questions or act out characters and events from a story or poem that is read aloud.
• Show interest in learning new vocabulary.
• Recognize the difference between different types of text.
• Draw pictures to make connections to the text or to themselves.
• Make connections between a story or poem and their experiences.
• Compare and contrast two stories about the same topic.
• Describe the role of the author and the illustrator.
• Participate in group literacy activities with purpose and understanding.

First Grade

Key Ideas and Details

• Ask and answer questions about key details in a text.
• Use key details to retell stories.
• Understand the message or lesson of a story.
• Use key details to describe characters, settings, and major events in a story.

Craft and Structure

• Identify words and phrases that suggest feelings or appeal to the senses.
• Explain differences between fiction and nonfiction books.
• Identify who is telling the story at various points in a text.

Integration of Knowledge and Ideas

• Use illustrations and details in a story to describe its characters, setting, or events.
• Compare and contrast the adventures and experiences of characters in stories.

Range of Reading and Level of Text Complexity

• Read prose and poetry of appropriate complexity for grade 1.

*Although Common Core State Standards are not yet available for prekindergarten, Pre-K students may be expected to demonstrate some level of competency for these skills.

Reading: Literature Concepts Checklist

Concept	Dates Taught				

Literature Comprehension

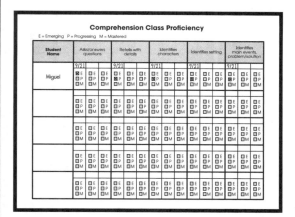

Use this page to track class proficiency levels in literature comprehension. Record student names in the left-hand column. Enter a level of mastery in the following columns. As you present the skills, record the date and mark *E, P,* or *M* (note the rating scale at the top of the page) to indicate the level of progress for each skill. This will allow you to see at a glance which students have mastered these skills and which students need help. Use this sheet as a reference tool for principal-teacher or grade-level meetings.

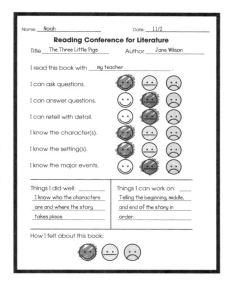

Use this page to conference with a student about how well she comprehended a fiction book or text. First, list the title and author of the book. After reading it with the student, discuss and rate how well she did for each skill listed. Point out any strengths or concepts the student needs to work on and list them in the corresponding sections of the page. Finally, have the student rate how she felt about the book or text. This page can also be used in a student's reading portfolio to show progress in literature comprehension.

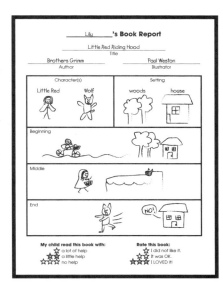

This page is ideal for sending home to show families their child's progress in retelling a story. Family members should be encouraged to read a fiction book to or with their student. Then, the student should fill out the book report with pictures or words. At the bottom, the family member should rate how well the child read the book. Then, the student should rate how he felt about the book.

Literature Comprehension Class Proficiency

E = Emerging   P = Progressing   M = Mastered

Student Name	Asks/answers questions			Retells with details			Identifies characters			Identifies setting			Identifies main events, problem/solution		
	☐E ☐P ☐M	☐E ☐P ☐M	☐E ☐P ☐M	☐E ☐P ☐M	☐E ☐P ☐M	☐E ☐P ☐M	☐E ☐P ☐M	☐E ☐P ☐M	☐E ☐P ☐M	☐E ☐P ☐M	☐E ☐P ☐M	☐E ☐P ☐M	☐E ☐P ☐M	☐E ☐P ☐M	☐E ☐P ☐M
	☐E ☐P ☐M	☐E ☐P ☐M	☐E ☐P ☐M	☐E ☐P ☐M	☐E ☐P ☐M	☐E ☐P ☐M	☐E ☐P ☐M	☐E ☐P ☐M	☐E ☐P ☐M	☐E ☐P ☐M	☐E ☐P ☐M	☐E ☐P ☐M	☐E ☐P ☐M	☐E ☐P ☐M	☐E ☐P ☐M
	☐E ☐P ☐M	☐E ☐P ☐M	☐E ☐P ☐M	☐E ☐P ☐M	☐E ☐P ☐M	☐E ☐P ☐M	☐E ☐P ☐M	☐E ☐P ☐M	☐E ☐P ☐M	☐E ☐P ☐M	☐E ☐P ☐M	☐E ☐P ☐M	☐E ☐P ☐M	☐E ☐P ☐M	☐E ☐P ☐M
	☐E ☐P ☐M	☐E ☐P ☐M	☐E ☐P ☐M	☐E ☐P ☐M	☐E ☐P ☐M	☐E ☐P ☐M	☐E ☐P ☐M	☐E ☐P ☐M	☐E ☐P ☐M	☐E ☐P ☐M	☐E ☐P ☐M	☐E ☐P ☐M	☐E ☐P ☐M	☐E ☐P ☐M	☐E ☐P ☐M
	☐E ☐P ☐M	☐E ☐P ☐M	☐E ☐P ☐M	☐E ☐P ☐M	☐E ☐P ☐M	☐E ☐P ☐M	☐E ☐P ☐M	☐E ☐P ☐M	☐E ☐P ☐M	☐E ☐P ☐M	☐E ☐P ☐M	☐E ☐P ☐M	☐E ☐P ☐M	☐E ☐P ☐M	☐E ☐P ☐M

Name: _____   Date: _____

Reading Conference for Literature

Title _____   Author _____

I read this book with _____ .

I can ask questions.

I can answer questions.

I can retell with detail.

I know the character(s).

I know the setting(s).

I know the major events.

Things I did well: _____	Things I can work on: _____
_____	_____
_____	_____
_____	_____

How I felt about this book:

_____'s Book Report

_____
Title

_____ _____
Author Illustrator

Character(s)	Setting

Beginning

Middle

End

My child read this book with:
☆ a lot of help
☆☆ a little help
☆☆☆ no help

Rate this book:
☆ I did not like it.
☆☆ It was OK.
☆☆☆ I LOVED it!

Tracking Reading

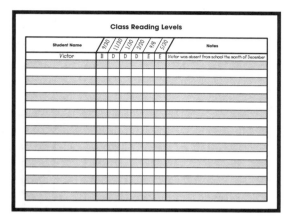

Use this page to access class reading levels at a glance. Record student names in the left-hand column. Throughout the year, note the date and the student's current reading level with the scale you prefer. Use the *Notes* section to record strengths, weaknesses, or concerns. Additionally, this page can be used to place students into reading groups.

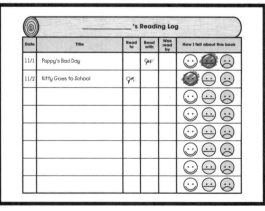

Use this page to record notes and observations in your reading groups. Record the title of the book you are reading with the group and the skill focus for that date. Record any notes in the *Notes* section. The bottom portion of the page is designed to record any concerns, strengths, or weaknesses for the individual students in the reading group. If desired, place self-stick notes in each block at the bottom of the page with the student's name and record any notes. Then, move the self-stick note with the observations to the student's reading portfolio to document reading progress.

Have students use this reading log to keep track of their independent fiction or nonfiction reading. The reading log can be used in the classroom or at home. The student, parent, or teacher should record the date and title of the book. The person the book is read to, with, or by should initial in the corresponding box. Then, the student should color the appropriate face to show how she felt about the book.

Class Reading Levels

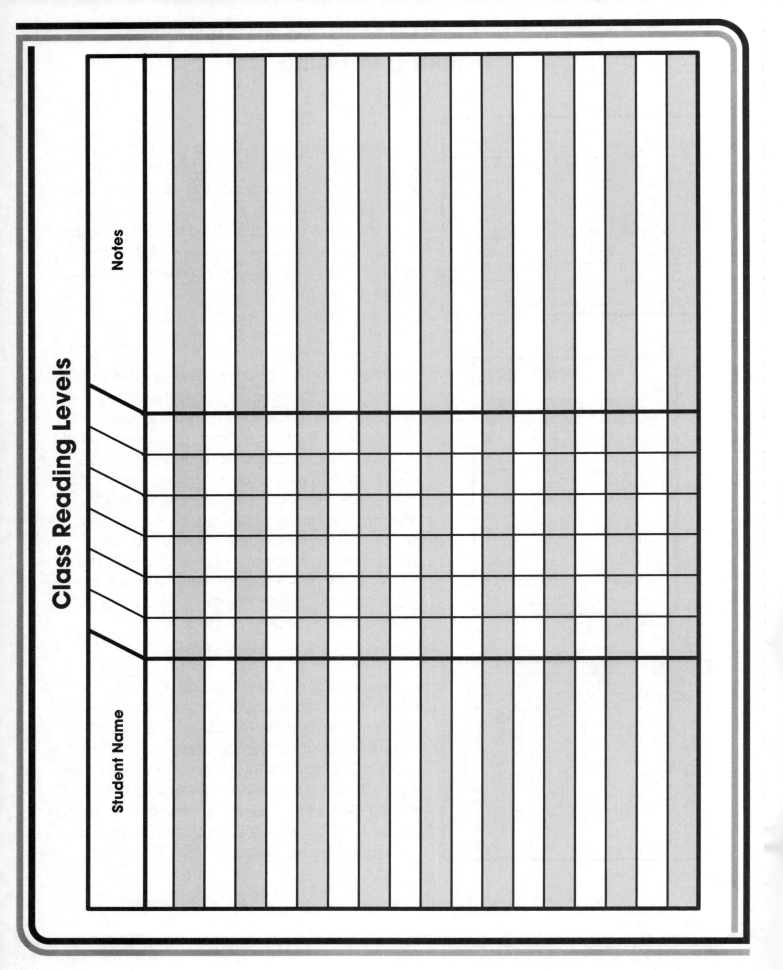

Student Name		Notes

Reading Group Observation

Group _____

Date	Title	Skill Focus	Notes

_____'s Reading Log

How I felt about this book	Was read by	Read with	Read to	Title	Date

Reading: Informational Text Standards Crosswalk

Prekindergarten*

Children should demonstrate increasing competency in the following, with prompting and support:

- Ask and answer questions about informational text read aloud.
- Recall important facts after hearing a text read aloud.
- Act out concepts learned from informational text.
- Show interest in learning new vocabulary.
- Handle books correctly, identifying their front and back covers.
- Describe details from a photo or illustration.
- Describe the roles of the author and the illustrator.
- Participate in group reading activities with purpose and understanding.

First Grade

Key Ideas and Details

- Ask and answer questions about key details in a text.
- Identify the main topic and retell key details of a text.
- Connect two individuals, events, ideas, or pieces of information in a text.

Craft and Structure

- Ask and answer questions to help understand the meaning of words and phrases.
- Know and use text features (headings, tables of contents, glossaries, electronic menus, icons) to locate key facts or information in a text.
- Distinguish information provided by visual aids from information provided by the words in a text.

Integration of Knowledge and Ideas

- Use the illustrations and details in a text to describe its key ideas.
- Identify the reasons an author gives to support points in a text.
- Identify basic similarities or differences between two texts on the same topic.

Range of Reading and Level of Text Complexity

- Read informational texts that are appropriately complex for grade 1.

*Although Common Core State Standards are not yet available for prekindergarten, Pre-K students may be expected to demonstrate some level of competency for these skills.

Reading: Informational Text Concepts Checklist

Concept	Dates Taught				

Informational Text Comprehension

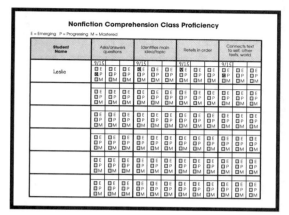

Use this page to track class proficiency levels in informational text comprehension. Record student names in the left-hand column. Enter a level of mastery in the following columns. As you present the skills, record the date and mark *E*, *P*, or *M* (note the rating scale at the top of the page) to indicate the progress of each skill. This will allow you to see at a glance which students have mastered these skills and which need help. Use this page as a reference tool for principal-teacher or grade-level meetings.

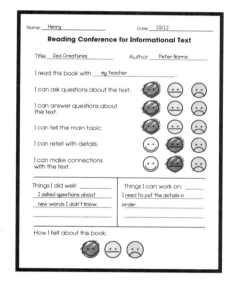

Use this page to conference with a student about how well he comprehended a nonfiction book or text. First, list the title and author of the informational text. After reading it with the student, discuss and rate how well he did for each skill listed. Point out any strengths or concepts the student needs to work on and list them in the corresponding sections of the page. Finally, have the student rate how he felt about the book or text. This page can also be used in a student's reading portfolio to show progress in nonfiction comprehension.

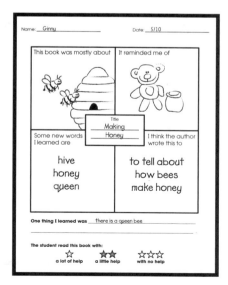

This page is ideal for sending home to show families their child's progress in comprehending informational text. Family members should be encouraged to read a nonfiction book to or with their student. Then, the student should fill out the graphic organizer with pictures or words. At the bottom, the student should write one thing she learned from the book. Finally, the family member should rate how well the child read the book.

Nonfiction Comprehension Class Proficiency

E = Emerging   P = Progressing   M = Mastered

Student Name	Asks/answers questions	Identifies main idea/topic	Retells in order	Connects text to self, other texts, world
	E ☐ P ☐ M ☐ E ☐ P ☐ M ☐ E ☐ P ☐ M ☐	E ☐ P ☐ M ☐ E ☐ P ☐ M ☐ E ☐ P ☐ M ☐	E ☐ P ☐ M ☐ E ☐ P ☐ M ☐ E ☐ P ☐ M ☐	E ☐ P ☐ M ☐ E ☐ P ☐ M ☐ E ☐ P ☐ M ☐
	E ☐ P ☐ M ☐ E ☐ P ☐ M ☐ E ☐ P ☐ M ☐	E ☐ P ☐ M ☐ E ☐ P ☐ M ☐ E ☐ P ☐ M ☐	E ☐ P ☐ M ☐ E ☐ P ☐ M ☐ E ☐ P ☐ M ☐	E ☐ P ☐ M ☐ E ☐ P ☐ M ☐ E ☐ P ☐ M ☐
	E ☐ P ☐ M ☐ E ☐ P ☐ M ☐ E ☐ P ☐ M ☐	E ☐ P ☐ M ☐ E ☐ P ☐ M ☐ E ☐ P ☐ M ☐	E ☐ P ☐ M ☐ E ☐ P ☐ M ☐ E ☐ P ☐ M ☐	E ☐ P ☐ M ☐ E ☐ P ☐ M ☐ E ☐ P ☐ M ☐
	E ☐ P ☐ M ☐ E ☐ P ☐ M ☐ E ☐ P ☐ M ☐	E ☐ P ☐ M ☐ E ☐ P ☐ M ☐ E ☐ P ☐ M ☐	E ☐ P ☐ M ☐ E ☐ P ☐ M ☐ E ☐ P ☐ M ☐	E ☐ P ☐ M ☐ E ☐ P ☐ M ☐ E ☐ P ☐ M ☐
	E ☐ P ☐ M ☐ E ☐ P ☐ M ☐ E ☐ P ☐ M ☐	E ☐ P ☐ M ☐ E ☐ P ☐ M ☐ E ☐ P ☐ M ☐	E ☐ P ☐ M ☐ E ☐ P ☐ M ☐ E ☐ P ☐ M ☐	E ☐ P ☐ M ☐ E ☐ P ☐ M ☐ E ☐ P ☐ M ☐
	E ☐ P ☐ M ☐ E ☐ P ☐ M ☐ E ☐ P ☐ M ☐	E ☐ P ☐ M ☐ E ☐ P ☐ M ☐ E ☐ P ☐ M ☐	E ☐ P ☐ M ☐ E ☐ P ☐ M ☐ E ☐ P ☐ M ☐	E ☐ P ☐ M ☐ E ☐ P ☐ M ☐ E ☐ P ☐ M ☐

Name: _____   Date: _____

Reading Conference for Informational Text

Title _____   Author _____

I read this book with _____ .

I can ask questions about the text.

I can answer questions about the text.

I can tell the main topic.

I can retell with details.

I can make connections with the text.

Things I did well: _____

_____

_____

_____

Things I can work on: _____

_____

_____

How I felt about this book:

Name: _____   Date: _____

This book was mostly about	It reminded me of

Title

_____

_____

Some new words I learned are	I think the author wrote this to

One thing I learned was _____

_____ .

The student read this book with:

☆   ☆☆   ☆☆☆
a lot of help   **a little help**   **no help**

Understanding Books

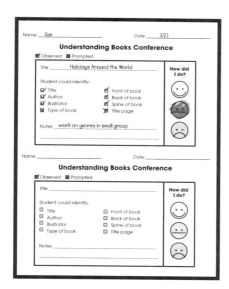

This page is perfect for conferencing with a student about how well they understand the structure of a book. Begin by showing a book to the student. Have the student point out the various elements of a book. Check the boxes (note the scoring marks at the top of the page) that apply. Use the *Notes* section to record any observations or concerns. The student should color a face to the right to show how she felt she did on the activity. This page can be used as a pretest and posttest assessment if desired.

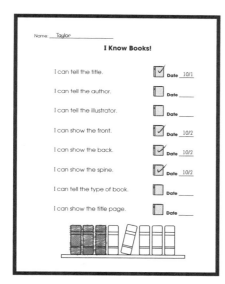

Use this page to help students show ownership of their understanding of the structure of books. Each time a student masters a concept he should write the date and place a check mark in the corresponding book. For each check mark, the student should color one of the books in the bookshelf at the bottom of the page.

This page is a fun, interactive way for students to track the genres of the books they read each month. The student should color one of the flower petals each time he reads that particular genre of book. If he runs out of petals on a flower (genre), encourage him to draw new petals. This also gives the teacher a quick snapshot of how many books of each genre the student is reading every month. Supply the student with a new page each month.

Name: _____ Date: _____

Understanding Books Conference

☑ Observed ☒ Prompted

Title _____

How did I do?

Student could identify:

☐ Title   ☐ Front of book
☐ Author   ☐ Back of book
☐ Illustrator   ☐ Spine of book
☐ Type of book   ☐ Title page

Notes _____

_____

Name: _____ Date: _____

Understanding Books Conference

☑ Observed ☒ Prompted

Title _____

How did I do?

Student could identify:

☐ Title   ☐ Front of book
☐ Author   ☐ Back of book
☐ Illustrator   ☐ Spine of book
☐ Type of book   ☐ Title page

Notes _____

_____

Name: _____

I Know Books!

I can tell the title.   Date _____

I can tell the author.   Date _____

I can tell the illustrator.   Date _____

I can show the front.   Date _____

I can show the back.   Date _____

I can show the spine.   Date _____

I can tell the type of book.   Date _____

I can show the title page.   Date _____

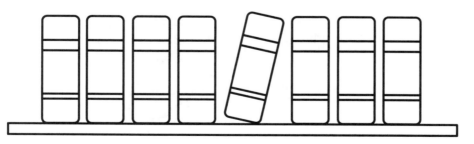

Name: _____

Month: _____

I Can Read Different Types of Books!

Fables

Tall Tales

Fairy Tales

Nonfiction

Fiction

Reading: Foundational Skills Standards Crosswalk

Prekindergarten*

Children should demonstrate increasing competency in the following with prompting and support:

• Understand that print can be read and has meaning.
• Follow words left to right, top to bottom, and page by page.
• Recognize some lower- and uppercase letters.
• Recognize and match rhyming words.
• Show awareness of the relationship between sounds and letters.
• Identify the beginning sound of a spoken word.
• Generate a list of words with the same initial sound.
• Show one-to-one letter/sound correspondence of some consonants.
• Recognize own name and some environmental print.
• Display beginning reading behaviors, such as pretend reading.

First Grade

Print Concepts

• Recognize the unique first word, capitalization, and punctuation of a sentence.

Phonological Awareness

• Demonstrate understanding of spoken words, syllables, and phonemes.
• Distinguish long from short vowel sounds in spoken single-syllable words.
• Orally blend sounds, including consonant blends, in single-syllable words.
• Isolate and pronounce initial, medial vowel, and final sounds in spoken single-syllable words.
• Segment spoken single-syllable words into all individual sounds.

Phonics and Word Recognition

• Decode words using grade-level phonics and word analysis skills.
• Know the spelling and sounds of common consonant digraphs.
• Decode regularly spelled one-syllable words.
• Know final -*e* and common vowel teams that produce long vowel sounds.
• Determine the number of syllables in a word by knowing that each syllable must have a vowel sound.
• Break words into known syllables to decode two-syllable words.
• Read words with inflectional endings.
• Recognize and read grade-appropriate, irregularly spelled words.

Fluency

• Read with accuracy and fluency to support comprehension.
• Read grade-level text with purpose and understanding.
• Read grade-level text orally with accuracy, fluency, and expression.
• Use context and rereading to confirm or self-correct understanding of text.

*Although Common Core State Standards are not yet available for prekindergarten, Pre-K students may be expected to demonstrate some level of competency for these skills.

Reading: Foundational Skills Concepts Checklist

Concept		Dates Taught				

Print Concepts

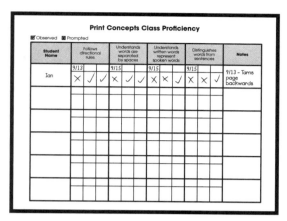

This page allows you to see at a glance where students are in their knowledge of print concepts. Record student names in the left-hand column. In the following columns, enter a level of mastery for each concept (note the scoring marks at the top of the page) and the date assessed. Use the *Notes* section to record any observations or concerns.

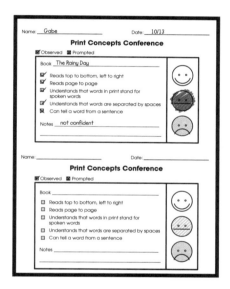

After you've introduced the elements of print concepts, use this conference sheet to allow students to show what they know. Write the title of the book. Show the book to the student. Observe how she reads or attempts to read the book. Then, assess each concept (note the scoring marks at the top). Use the *Notes* section to record any observations or concerns. Allow the student to color a face to the right to show how she felt about the activity. This page also can be used as a pretest and posttest assessment if desired.

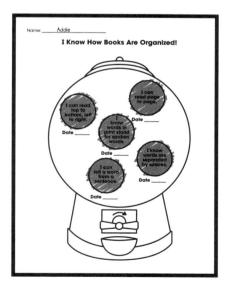

With this sheet, students can track their progress in learning print concepts. Have students color a piece of bubble gum to match each print concept that he masters. Have the student write the date he mastered each concept.

Print Concepts Class Proficiency

☑ Observed ☒ Prompted

Student Name	Follows directional rules			Understands words are separated by spaces			Understands written words represent spoken words			Distinguishes words from sentences			Notes

Name: _____ Date: _____

Print Concepts Conference

☑ Observed ☒ Prompted

Book _____

- ☐ Reads top to bottom, left to right
- ☐ Reads page to page
- ☐ Understands that words in print stand for spoken words
- ☐ Understands that words are separated by spaces
- ☐ Can tell a word from a sentence

Notes _____

_____

Name: _____ Date: _____

Print Concepts Conference

☑ Observed ☒ Prompted

Book _____

- ☐ Reads top to bottom, left to right
- ☐ Reads page to page
- ☐ Understands that words in print stand for spoken words
- ☐ Understands that words are separated by spaces
- ☐ Can tell a word from a sentence

Notes _____

_____

Name: _____

I Know How Books Are Organized!

I can read top to bottom, left to right.

Date _____

I can read page to page.

Date _____

I know words in print stand for spoken words.

Date _____

I know words are separated by spaces.

Date _____

I can tell a word from a sentence.

Date _____

Letter/Sound Recognition

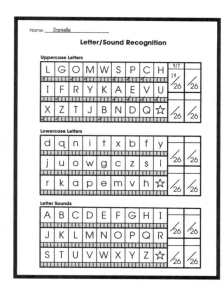

Use this page to individually assess each student's ability to recognize uppercase and lowercase letters and the sounds associated with them. For each assessment, place a check mark in the box under each letter that the student recognizes or sounds out. Record the date and the score in the right-hand columns each time. When all of the letters and sounds have been identified, have the student color the star at the end of the last row.

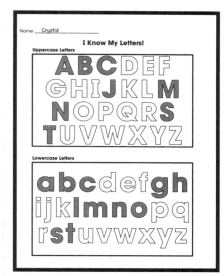

Students should keep this page to record their progress over time as they master letter recognition. Have students color each uppercase letter and lowercase letter as they master recognition of it.

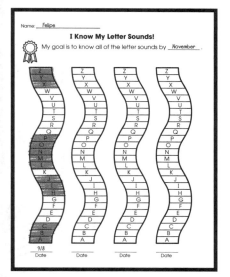

This page allows students to track their progress and take ownership of recoginizing letters and sounds. First, have students set a goal for when they want to know all of their letter sounds. Then, color the corresponding letter sounds they have mastered for each date assessed.

Name: _____

Letter/Sound Recognition

Uppercase Letters

L	G	O	M	W	S	P	C	H	/26	/26
I	F	R	Y	K	A	E	V	U		
X	Z	T	J	B	N	D	Q	☆	/26	/26

Lowercase Letters

d	a	n	i	t	x	b	f	y	/26	/26
j	u	o	w	g	c	z	s	l		
r	k	a	p	e	m	v	h	☆	/26	/26

Letter Sounds

A	B	C	D	E	F	G	H	I	/26	/26
J	K	L	M	N	O	P	Q	R		
S	T	U	V	W	X	Y	Z	☆	/26	/26

Name: _____

I Know My Letters!

Uppercase Letters

A B C D E F
G H I J K L M
N O P Q R S
T U V W X Y Z

Lowercase Letters

a b c d e f g h
i j k l m n o p q
r s t u v w x y z

Name: _____

I Know My Letter Sounds!

My goal is to know all of the letter sounds by _____ .

Z	Z	Z	Z
Y	Y	Y	Y
X	X	X	X
W	W	W	W
V	V	V	V
U	U	U	U
T	T	T	T
S	S	S	S
R	R	R	R
Q	Q	Q	Q
P	P	P	P
O	O	O	O
N	N	N	N
M	M	M	M
L	L	L	L
K	K	K	K
J	J	J	J
I	I	I	I
H	H	H	H
G	G	G	G
F	F	F	F
E	E	E	E
D	D	D	D
C	C	C	C
B	B	B	B
A	A	A	A

Date _____ Date _____ Date _____ Date _____

Phonemic Awareness

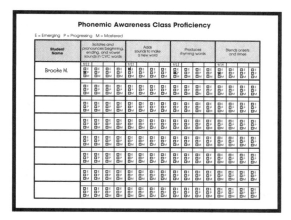

Use this page to keep track of your class's proficiency in phonemic awareness skills. Record student names in the left-hand column. As you present the skills, record the date and mark *E*, *P*, or *M* (note the rating scale at the top of the page) to indicate the progress of each skill. Present this page at principal-teacher conferences or grade-level meetings to quickly show how your students are progressing in the area of phonemic awareness skills.

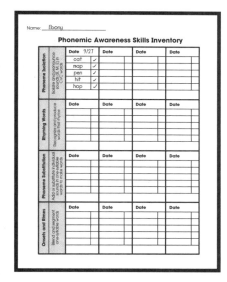

Use this skills inventory page to assess students' more closely in the area of phonemic awareness. Before the assessment, choose various CVC words that correspond with each skill set on the page. Type or write them on index cards. Record the date and the words used for the assessment in the first column. Then, as you present a student with words, record how she performed in the appropriate space on the chart using a check mark system. Use the blank space at the bottom of each section to record any additional observations.

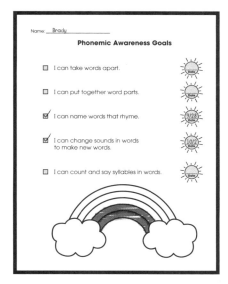

This page is useful for allowing students to track progress of their phonemic awareness goals throughout the school year. As the student masters each skill he should write the date he achieved the goal and then color one arch of the rainbow. The rainbow will be completely colored after all of the student's goals have been attained.

Phonemic Awareness Class Proficiency

E = Emerging   P = Progressing   M = Mastered

Student Name	Isolates and pronounces beginning, ending, and vowel sounds in CVC words				Adds sounds to make a new word				Produces rhyming words				Blends onsets and rimes			
	E ☐ P ☐ M ☐	E ☐ P ☐ M ☐	E ☐ P ☐ M ☐	E ☐ P ☐ M ☐	E ☐ P ☐ M ☐	E ☐ P ☐ M ☐	E ☐ P ☐ M ☐	E ☐ P ☐ M ☐	E ☐ P ☐ M ☐	E ☐ P ☐ M ☐	E ☐ P ☐ M ☐	E ☐ P ☐ M ☐	E ☐ P ☐ M ☐	E ☐ P ☐ M ☐	E ☐ P ☐ M ☐	E ☐ P ☐ M ☐
	E ☐ P ☐ M ☐	E ☐ P ☐ M ☐	E ☐ P ☐ M ☐	E ☐ P ☐ M ☐	E ☐ P ☐ M ☐	E ☐ P ☐ M ☐	E ☐ P ☐ M ☐	E ☐ P ☐ M ☐	E ☐ P ☐ M ☐	E ☐ P ☐ M ☐	E ☐ P ☐ M ☐	E ☐ P ☐ M ☐	E ☐ P ☐ M ☐	E ☐ P ☐ M ☐	E ☐ P ☐ M ☐	E ☐ P ☐ M ☐
	E ☐ P ☐ M ☐	E ☐ P ☐ M ☐	E ☐ P ☐ M ☐	E ☐ P ☐ M ☐	E ☐ P ☐ M ☐	E ☐ P ☐ M ☐	E ☐ P ☐ M ☐	E ☐ P ☐ M ☐	E ☐ P ☐ M ☐	E ☐ P ☐ M ☐	E ☐ P ☐ M ☐	E ☐ P ☐ M ☐	E ☐ P ☐ M ☐	E ☐ P ☐ M ☐	E ☐ P ☐ M ☐	E ☐ P ☐ M ☐
	E ☐ P ☐ M ☐	E ☐ P ☐ M ☐	E ☐ P ☐ M ☐	E ☐ P ☐ M ☐	E ☐ P ☐ M ☐	E ☐ P ☐ M ☐	E ☐ P ☐ M ☐	E ☐ P ☐ M ☐	E ☐ P ☐ M ☐	E ☐ P ☐ M ☐	E ☐ P ☐ M ☐	E ☐ P ☐ M ☐	E ☐ P ☐ M ☐	E ☐ P ☐ M ☐	E ☐ P ☐ M ☐	E ☐ P ☐ M ☐
	E ☐ P ☐ M ☐	E ☐ P ☐ M ☐	E ☐ P ☐ M ☐	E ☐ P ☐ M ☐	E ☐ P ☐ M ☐	E ☐ P ☐ M ☐	E ☐ P ☐ M ☐	E ☐ P ☐ M ☐	E ☐ P ☐ M ☐	E ☐ P ☐ M ☐	E ☐ P ☐ M ☐	E ☐ P ☐ M ☐	E ☐ P ☐ M ☐	E ☐ P ☐ M ☐	E ☐ P ☐ M ☐	E ☐ P ☐ M ☐
	E ☐ P ☐ M ☐	E ☐ P ☐ M ☐	E ☐ P ☐ M ☐	E ☐ P ☐ M ☐	E ☐ P ☐ M ☐	E ☐ P ☐ M ☐	E ☐ P ☐ M ☐	E ☐ P ☐ M ☐	E ☐ P ☐ M ☐	E ☐ P ☐ M ☐	E ☐ P ☐ M ☐	E ☐ P ☐ M ☐	E ☐ P ☐ M ☐	E ☐ P ☐ M ☐	E ☐ P ☐ M ☐	E ☐ P ☐ M ☐
	E ☐ P ☐ M ☐	E ☐ P ☐ M ☐	E ☐ P ☐ M ☐	E ☐ P ☐ M ☐	E ☐ P ☐ M ☐	E ☐ P ☐ M ☐	E ☐ P ☐ M ☐	E ☐ P ☐ M ☐	E ☐ P ☐ M ☐	E ☐ P ☐ M ☐	E ☐ P ☐ M ☐	E ☐ P ☐ M ☐	E ☐ P ☐ M ☐	E ☐ P ☐ M ☐	E ☐ P ☐ M ☐	E ☐ P ☐ M ☐
	E ☐ P ☐ M ☐	E ☐ P ☐ M ☐	E ☐ P ☐ M ☐	E ☐ P ☐ M ☐	E ☐ P ☐ M ☐	E ☐ P ☐ M ☐	E ☐ P ☐ M ☐	E ☐ P ☐ M ☐	E ☐ P ☐ M ☐	E ☐ P ☐ M ☐	E ☐ P ☐ M ☐	E ☐ P ☐ M ☐	E ☐ P ☐ M ☐	E ☐ P ☐ M ☐	E ☐ P ☐ M ☐	E ☐ P ☐ M ☐

Name: _____

Phonemic Awareness Skills Inventory

Phoneme Isolation	Isolate and pronounce sounds (B, M, E) in CVC words	Date		Date		Date		Date	

Rhyming Words	Recognize and produce words that rhyme	Date		Date		Date		Date	

Phoneme Substitution	Add or substitute individual sounds in one-syllable words to make words	Date		Date		Date		Date	

Onsets and Rimes	Blend and segment one-syllable words	Date		Date		Date		Date	

Name: _____

Phonemic Awareness Goals

☐ I can take words apart.

☐ I can put together word parts.

☐ I can name words that rhyme.

☐ I can change sounds in words
to make new words.

☐ I can count and say syllables in words.

Decoding Skills

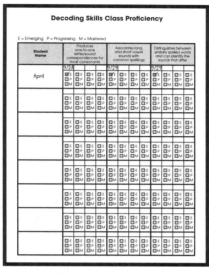

Decoding Skills Class Proficiency

E = Emerging P = Progressing M = Mastered

Student Name	Produces one-to-one letter/sound correspondences for most consonants			Associates long and short vowel sounds with common spellings			Distinguishes between similarly spelled words and can identify the sounds that differ		
	9/28			9/29			9/29		
April	☑E ☐P ☐M	☐E ☐P ☐M	☐E ☐P ☐M	☑E ☐P ☐M	☐E ☐P ☐M	☐E ☐P ☐M	☑E ☐P ☐M	☐E ☐P ☐M	☐E ☐P ☐M
	☐E ☐P ☐M	☐E ☐P ☐M	☐E ☐P ☐M	☐E ☐P ☐M	☐E ☐P ☐M	☐E ☐P ☐M	☐E ☐P ☐M	☐E ☐P ☐M	☐E ☐P ☐M
	☐E ☐P ☐M	☐E ☐P ☐M	☐E ☐P ☐M	☐E ☐P ☐M	☐E ☐P ☐M	☐E ☐P ☐M	☐E ☐P ☐M	☐E ☐P ☐M	☐E ☐P ☐M
	☐E ☐P ☐M	☐E ☐P ☐M	☐E ☐P ☐M	☐E ☐P ☐M	☐E ☐P ☐M	☐E ☐P ☐M	☐E ☐P ☐M	☐E ☐P ☐M	☐E ☐P ☐M
	☐E ☐P ☐M	☐E ☐P ☐M	☐E ☐P ☐M	☐E ☐P ☐M	☐E ☐P ☐M	☐E ☐P ☐M	☐E ☐P ☐M	☐E ☐P ☐M	☐E ☐P ☐M
	☐E ☐P ☐M	☐E ☐P ☐M	☐E ☐P ☐M	☐E ☐P ☐M	☐E ☐P ☐M	☐E ☐P ☐M	☐E ☐P ☐M	☐E ☐P ☐M	☐E ☐P ☐M
	☐E ☐P ☐M	☐E ☐P ☐M	☐E ☐P ☐M	☐E ☐P ☐M	☐E ☐P ☐M	☐E ☐P ☐M	☐E ☐P ☐M	☐E ☐P ☐M	☐E ☐P ☐M
	☐E ☐P ☐M	☐E ☐P ☐M	☐E ☐P ☐M	☐E ☐P ☐M	☐E ☐P ☐M	☐E ☐P ☐M	☐E ☐P ☐M	☐E ☐P ☐M	☐E ☐P ☐M

Use this form to keep record of your entire class's proficiency in decoding skills. Record student names in the left-hand column. As you present the skills, record the date and mark *E, P,* or *M* (note the rating scale at the top of the page) to indicate the progress of each skill. This chart is perfect for planning small group instruction.

Name: _Liz_

Decoding Assessment

Date: _10/1_

	CVC Pattern	Correct	Incorrect	Did not try	
Real Words	has	✓			☑ Pronounces each sound, then blends
	fub	✓			☐ Quick
	wig		✓		☐ Slow
	net	✓			Notes
	hog	✓			
Nonsense Words	lim	✓			
	vug	✓			
	fep			✓	
	waz			✓	
	hov			✓	

Date: _____

	CVC Pattern	Correct	Incorrect	Did not try	
Real Words					☐ Pronounces each sound, then blends
					☐ Quick
					☐ Slow
					Notes
Nonsense Words					

Use this page to assess each student's word decoding skills more closely. Before the assessment, chose CVC words (nonsense and real) and write or type them on a page or index cards. Record the words used for the assessment in the first column. As you present the student with words, record how she performed in the appropriate spaces on the chart using a check mark system. In the last column, note how the student responded to the set of words. Use the *Notes* section to record any additional observations.

Decoding Scores

Student Name	Date	Score	Date	Score	Date	Score	Date	Score
Clarke	9/1	7/10	12/2	9/15	2/12	9/15	5/2	12/20
Brent	9/2	8/10	12/3	9/15	2/12	11/15	5/2	18/20
		/		/		/		/
		/		/		/		/
		/		/		/		/
		/		/		/		/
		/		/		/		/
		/		/		/		/
		/		/		/		/
		/		/		/		/
		/		/		/		/
		/		/		/		/
		/		/		/		/
		/		/		/		/
		/		/		/		/
		/		/		/		/

Use this page to see assessment scores on decoding skills for your class at a glance. As you assess students on decoding isolated words or when reading a passage, record the date and the amount of correct words out of the total number of words assessed. You may assess each student up to three times throughout the year with this page.

Decoding Skills Class Proficiency

E = Emerging   P = Progressing   M = Mastered

Student Name	Produces one-to-one letter/sound correspondences for most consonants				Associates long and short vowel sounds with common spellings				Distinguishes between similarly spelled words and can identify the sounds that differ			
	☐E ☐P ☐M	☐E ☐P ☐M	☐E ☐P ☐M	☐E ☐P ☐M	☐E ☐P ☐M	☐E ☐P ☐M	☐E ☐P ☐M	☐E ☐P ☐M	☐E ☐P ☐M	☐E ☐P ☐M	☐E ☐P ☐M	☐E ☐P ☐M
	☐E ☐P ☐M	☐E ☐P ☐M	☐E ☐P ☐M	☐E ☐P ☐M	☐E ☐P ☐M	☐E ☐P ☐M	☐E ☐P ☐M	☐E ☐P ☐M	☐E ☐P ☐M	☐E ☐P ☐M	☐E ☐P ☐M	☐E ☐P ☐M
	☐E ☐P ☐M	☐E ☐P ☐M	☐E ☐P ☐M	☐E ☐P ☐M	☐E ☐P ☐M	☐E ☐P ☐M	☐E ☐P ☐M	☐E ☐P ☐M	☐E ☐P ☐M	☐E ☐P ☐M	☐E ☐P ☐M	☐E ☐P ☐M
	☐E ☐P ☐M	☐E ☐P ☐M	☐E ☐P ☐M	☐E ☐P ☐M	☐E ☐P ☐M	☐E ☐P ☐M	☐E ☐P ☐M	☐E ☐P ☐M	☐E ☐P ☐M	☐E ☐P ☐M	☐E ☐P ☐M	☐E ☐P ☐M
	☐E ☐P ☐M	☐E ☐P ☐M	☐E ☐P ☐M	☐E ☐P ☐M	☐E ☐P ☐M	☐E ☐P ☐M	☐E ☐P ☐M	☐E ☐P ☐M	☐E ☐P ☐M	☐E ☐P ☐M	☐E ☐P ☐M	☐E ☐P ☐M
	☐E ☐P ☐M	☐E ☐P ☐M	☐E ☐P ☐M	☐E ☐P ☐M	☐E ☐P ☐M	☐E ☐P ☐M	☐E ☐P ☐M	☐E ☐P ☐M	☐E ☐P ☐M	☐E ☐P ☐M	☐E ☐P ☐M	☐E ☐P ☐M
	☐E ☐P ☐M	☐E ☐P ☐M	☐E ☐P ☐M	☐E ☐P ☐M	☐E ☐P ☐M	☐E ☐P ☐M	☐E ☐P ☐M	☐E ☐P ☐M	☐E ☐P ☐M	☐E ☐P ☐M	☐E ☐P ☐M	☐E ☐P ☐M
	☐E ☐P ☐M	☐E ☐P ☐M	☐E ☐P ☐M	☐E ☐P ☐M	☐E ☐P ☐M	☐E ☐P ☐M	☐E ☐P ☐M	☐E ☐P ☐M	☐E ☐P ☐M	☐E ☐P ☐M	☐E ☐P ☐M	☐E ☐P ☐M

Name: _____

Decoding Skills Assessment

Date: _____

	CVC Pattern	Correct	Incorrect	Did not try	
Real Words					☐ Pronounces each sound, then blends
					☐ Quick
					☐ Slow
					Notes
Nonsense Words					

Date: _____

	CVC Pattern	Correct	Incorrect	Did not try	
Real Words					☐ Pronounces each sound, then blends
					☐ Quick
					☐ Slow
					Notes
Nonsense Words					

Decoding Skills Scores

Student Name	Date	Score	Date	Score	Date	Score	Date	Score
		/		/		/		/
		/		/		/		/
		/		/		/		/
		/		/		/		/
		/		/		/		/
		/		/		/		/
		/		/		/		/
		/		/		/		/
		/		/		/		/
		/		/		/		/
		/		/		/		/
		/		/		/		/
		/		/		/		/
		/		/		/		/
		/		/		/		/
		/		/		/		/
		/		/		/		/
		/		/		/		/
		/		/		/		/
		/		/		/		/

Short and Long Vowel Sounds

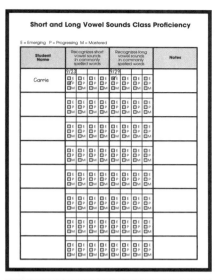

Use this page to record your class's proficiency in hearing and recognizing short and long vowel sounds in words. Record student names in the left-hand column. As you present the skills, record the date and mark *E*, *P*, or *M* (note the rating scale at the top of the page) to indicate the progress of each skill. This chart is perfect for presenting at principal-teacher conferences or grade-level meetings to quickly show how your students are progressing in vowel sound skills.

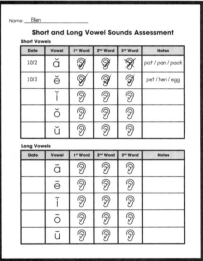

This page can be used to show student progress in recognizing long and short vowels sounds. For each vowel sound, say three words, one at a time, to the student. If the student can tell you he hears the vowel sound and can correctly identify it, place a check mark over the ear or have the student color the ear. Place an *X* over the ear if he does not correctly identify the vowel sound in the word. In the *Notes* section, you may write the words presented or note any observations.

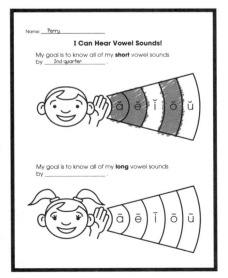

This page allows students to track their progress in recognizing long and short vowel sounds. Each student should first set a goal for when they want to know all of the long and short vowel sounds. As the student masters each vowel sound, she should color the corresponding sound wave.

Short and Long Vowel Sounds Class Proficiency

E = Emerging   P = Progressing   M = Mastered

Student Name	Recognizes short vowel sounds in commonly spelled words				Recognizes long vowel sounds in commonly spelled words				Notes
	□ E □ P □ M	□ E □ P □ M	□ E □ P □ M	□ E □ P □ M	□ E □ P □ M	□ E □ P □ M	□ E □ P □ M	□ E □ P □ M	
	□ E □ P □ M	□ E □ P □ M	□ E □ P □ M	□ E □ P □ M	□ E □ P □ M	□ E □ P □ M	□ E □ P □ M	□ E □ P □ M	
	□ E □ P □ M	□ E □ P □ M	□ E □ P □ M	□ E □ P □ M	□ E □ P □ M	□ E □ P □ M	□ E □ P □ M	□ E □ P □ M	
	□ E □ P □ M	□ E □ P □ M	□ E □ P □ M	□ E □ P □ M	□ E □ P □ M	□ E □ P □ M	□ E □ P □ M	□ E □ P □ M	
	□ E □ P □ M	□ E □ P □ M	□ E □ P □ M	□ E □ P □ M	□ E □ P □ M	□ E □ P □ M	□ E □ P □ M	□ E □ P □ M	
	□ E □ P □ M	□ E □ P □ M	□ E □ P □ M	□ E □ P □ M	□ E □ P □ M	□ E □ P □ M	□ E □ P □ M	□ E □ P □ M	
	□ E □ P □ M	□ E □ P □ M	□ E □ P □ M	□ E □ P □ M	□ E □ P □ M	□ E □ P □ M	□ E □ P □ M	□ E □ P □ M	
	□ E □ P □ M	□ E □ P □ M	□ E □ P □ M	□ E □ P □ M	□ E □ P □ M	□ E □ P □ M	□ E □ P □ M	□ E □ P □ M	

Name: _____

Short and Long Vowel Sounds Assessment

Short Vowels

Date	Vowel	1st Word	2nd Word	3rd Word	Notes
	ă				
	ĕ				
	ĭ				
	ŏ				
	ŭ				

Long Vowels

Date	Vowel	1st Word	2nd Word	3rd Word	Notes
	ā				
	ē				
	ī				
	ō				
	ū				

Name: _____

I Can Hear Vowel Sounds!

My goal is to know all of my **short** vowel sounds
by _____ .

My goal is to know all of my **long** vowel sounds
by _____ .

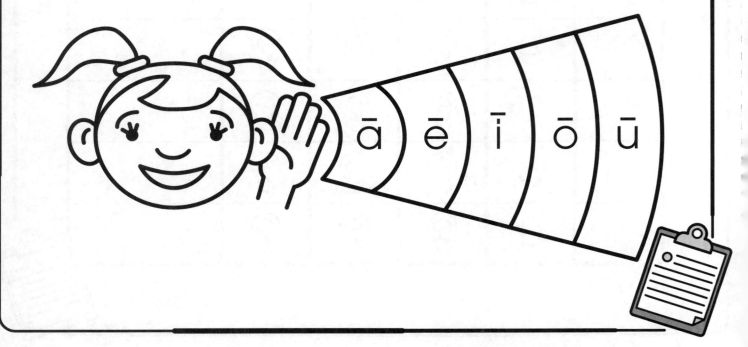

Sight Words

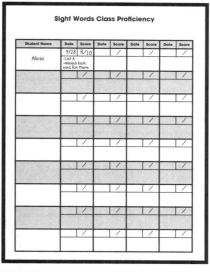

Use this page to record sight word assessment scores. After each assessment, record the date and the score. This allows you to see your entire class's sight word proficiency at a glance. Use the blank space in each row to record any notes or observations.

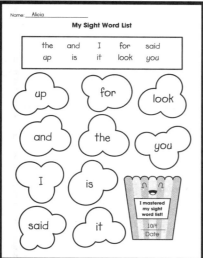

This page allows students to take pride and ownership in how well they know their sight words. Write the student's sight words in the blank box. Have the student read her sight word list for the week and then write each word in a piece of popcorn if she reads it correctly. At the end of the week, or when the student has mastered the sight word list, she should write the date in the popcorn box.

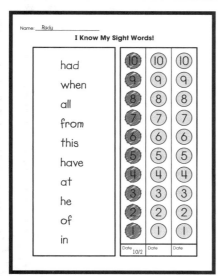

This page will allow the student to highlight his sight word progress over three dates. Present a list of 10 sight words. The student should copy the list of words in the blank section. Then, have the student graph the number of sight words he reads correctly on each specified date.

Sight Words Class Proficiency

Student Name	Date	Score	Date	Score	Date	Score	Date	Score
		/		/		/		/
		/		/		/		/
		/		/		/		/
		/		/		/		/
		/		/		/		/
		/		/		/		/
		/		/		/		/
		/		/		/		/

Name: _____

My Sight Word List

I mastered
my sight
word list!

Date

Name: _____

I Know My Sight Words!

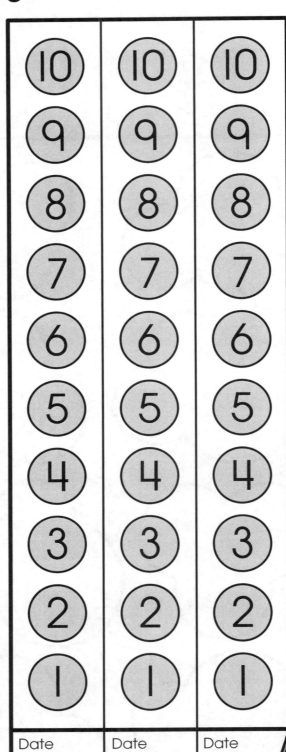

Fluency

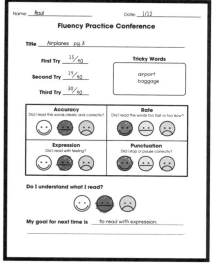

This page allows the student to rate his progress on the four main elements of oral fluency: expression, rate, punctuation, and accuracy. Present the student with a short passage to read. Each time the student reads the passage, record the number of words that were read correctly. Record any tricky words that the student struggled with. Then, the student should color a face to express how he felt about each element of his fluency practice. Finally, the student should color a face to show how he felt about his comprehension of the passage and set a goal for the next time he reads for fluency practice.

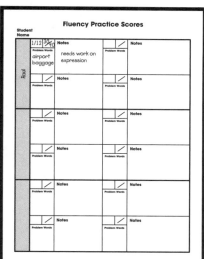

This page allows you to pinpoint progress for each student in the area of oral fluency. Give a student a short passage to read on four different occasions. Record the student's name in the far left column. Record the date and the fluency score each time a student reads a passage. Problem words can also be noted. Use the **Notes** section to record any observations. Fluency can be rated four times a year for each student, making the level of progress (or lack of progress) apparent.

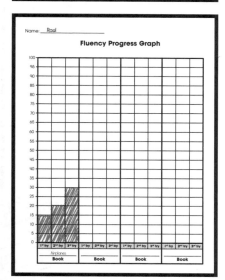

This page will allow the student to track her progress in reading fluently. For each practice, write the name of the book and record the number of words read correctly each time by coloring in the bar graph. It is recommended that you use a different color for each try to easily see progress in the same book.

Name: _____   Date: _____

Fluency Practice Conference

Title _____

First Try ____/____

Second Try ____/____

Third Try ____/____

Tricky Words

Accuracy	**Rate**
Did I read the words clearly and correctly?	Did I read the words too fast or too slow?
Expression	**Punctuation**
Did I read with feeling?	Did I stop or pause correctly?

Do I understand what I read?

My goal for next time is _____

_____

Fluency Practice Scores

Student Name

	/	**Notes**	/	**Notes**
	Problem Words		**Problem Words**	
	/	**Notes**	/	**Notes**
	Problem Words		**Problem Words**	
	/	**Notes**	/	**Notes**
	Problem Words		**Problem Words**	
	/	**Notes**	/	**Notes**
	Problem Words		**Problem Words**	
	/	**Notes**	/	**Notes**
	Problem Words		**Problem Words**	
	/	**Notes**	/	**Notes**
	Problem Words		**Problem Words**	

Name: _____

Fluency Progress Graph

	1st try	2nd try	3rd try		1st try	2nd try	3rd try		1st try	2nd try	3rd try		1st try	2nd try	3rd try
100															
95															
90															
85															
80															
75															
70															
65															
60															
55															
50															
45															
40															
35															
30															
25															
20															
15															
10															
5															
0	1st try	2nd try	3rd try		1st try	2nd try	3rd try		1st try	2nd try	3rd try		1st try	2nd try	3rd try

Book _____   Book _____   Book _____   Book _____

Writing
Standards Crosswalk

Prekindergarten*

Children should demonstrate increasing competency in the following, with prompting and support:

- Use drawing, dictating, or writing to express an opinion about a book or topic.
- Use drawing, dictating, or writing to compose informative or explanatory text that supplies information about a topic.
- Use drawing, dictating, or writing to narrate an event and tell how they feel about it.
- Respond to questions and suggestions to make illustrations or writing clearer.
- Recall information from a previous experience to answer a question.
- Participate in shared writing and research projects.

First Grade

Text Types and Purposes

- Write an opinion piece on a topic or book, and provide a reason and a closing.
- Write informative/explanatory text in which they name a topic, give facts about the topic, and provide a closing.
- Write a narrative recounting two or more sequenced events that uses details, order words, and provides a closing.

Production and Distribution of Writing

With guidance and support:

- Focus on a topic, respond to feedback from peers, and add details to strengthen writing.
- Use a variety of digital tools to produce and publish writing, including in collaboration with peers.

Research to Build and Present Knowledge

- Participate in shared research and writing projects.
- With guidance and support, recall information or gather information to answer a question.

*Although Common Core State Standards are not yet available for prekindergarten, Pre-K students may be expected to demonstrate some level of competency for these skills.

Writing Skills Concepts Checklist

Concept		Dates Taught				

Writing Skills

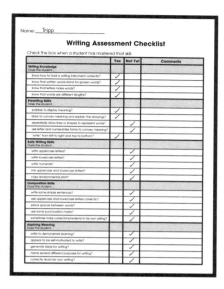

Use this writing assessment checklist to keep track of each student's mastery of writing skills. It can be also be used as a helpful tool when conferencing with a student or parent about writing expectations.

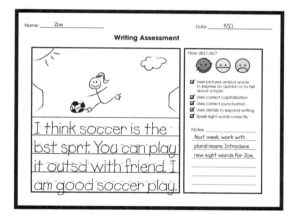

Use this page to guide a writing conference with each student. Have the student write a narrative, informational, or opinion piece in the box on the left. Ask her to draw a picture to go along with her writing. Use the checklist on the right to provide feedback to the student. Then, have the student color a face that shows how she felt she did on the assessment. Record any observations or concerns in the *Notes* section. This assessment makes an excellent portfolio or parent-conference piece.

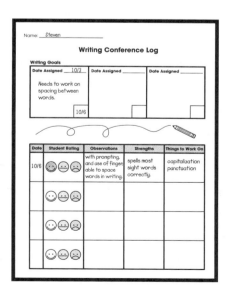

Use this page to conference with and assign writing goals to each student. In the first section of the page, assign writing goals as needed. After each writing assignment, read the piece the student wrote together and point out any goals that the student attained in his writing. Date the small box in the writing goals section as the student masters each goal. In the bottom chart, record the date of the conference and any strengths or weaknesses. Also, note skills the student should work on next time and have him color a face that shows how he felt about his writing.

Name: _____

Writing Assessment Checklist

Check the box when a student has mastered that skill.

	Yes	Not Yet	Comments
Writing Knowledge Does the student...			
know how to hold a writing instrument correctly?			
know that written words stand for spoken words?			
know that letters make words?			
know that words are different lengths?			
Prewriting Skills Does the student...			
scribble to display meaning?			
draw to convey meaning and explain the drawings?			
repeatedly draw lines or shapes to represent words?			
use letter and numeral-like forms to convey meaning?			
"write" from left to right and top to bottom?			
Early Writing Skills Does the student...			
write uppercase letters?			
write lowercase letters?			
write numerals?			
mix uppercase and lowercase letters?			
copy environmental print?			
Composition Skills Does the student...			
write some simple sentences?			
use uppercase and lowercase letters correctly?			
place spaces between words?			
use some punctuation marks?			
sometimes make corrections/revisions to his own writing?			
Applying Meaning Does the student...			
write to demonstrate learning?			
appear to be self-motivated to write?			
generate ideas for writing?			
name several different purposes for writing?			
correctly read her own writing?			

Writing Assessment

Name: _____

Date: _____

How did I do?

- ⊘ (grey circle with vertical line/frown)
- ⊗ (hatched circle with vertical line)
- ☺ (smiley face)

- ☐ Uses pictures and/or words to express an opinion or to tell about a topic
- ☐ Uses correct capitalization
- ☐ Uses correct punctuation
- ☐ Uses details to expand writing
- ☐ Spells sight words correctly

Notes _____
_____
_____
_____
_____
_____

Name: _____

Writing Skills Conference Log

Writing Goals

Date Assigned _____	Date Assigned _____	Date Assigned _____

Date	Student Rating	Observations	Strengths	Things to Work On
	☺ 😐 ☹			
	☺ 😐 ☹			
	☺ 😐 ☹			
	☺ 😐 ☹			

Speaking and Listening
Standards Crosswalk

Prekindergarten*
Children should demonstrate increasing competency in the following, with prompting and support:
- Interact in conversations with diverse partners during daily routines and play.
- Use appropriate methods of group conversation such as waiting their turn to speak.
- Continue a conversation through several exchanges.
- Recall information for short periods of time from information presented through a book, recording, or video, and retell the information.
- Ask and answer questions to clarify, seek help, or get information.
- Describe real or imagined personal experiences.
- Create visual displays to represent stories or experiences.
- Speak audibly and express thoughts, feelings, and ideas.

First Grade
Comprehension and Collaboration
- Participate in group discussions about grade-appropriate topics and texts.
- Follow agreed-upon discussion rules.
- Respond to remarks of others.
- Ask for clarification if needed.
- Ask and answer questions about key details in a text or other channels of information.
- Ask and answer questions about what a speaker says to better understand something.

Presentation of Knowledge and Ideas
- Use relevant details, ideas, and feelings to describe people, places, things, and events.
- Add visual displays to clarify descriptions when appropriate.
- Produce complete sentences when appropriate.

*Although Common Core State Standards are not yet available for prekindergarten, Pre-K students may be expected to demonstrate some level of competency for these skills.

Speaking and Listening Concepts Checklist

	Concept	Dates Taught				

Speaking and Listening Skills

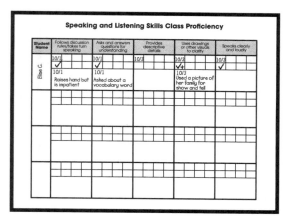

Use this page to keep track of your class's proficiency in speaking and listening skills. Record student names in the left-hand column. Each time you assess a student on a particular skill, use a check mark system to record their proficiency in that skill for the date observed. Make any notes or observations in the blank space in each row.

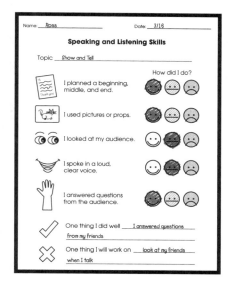

Use this page to help students self-assess their performance in discussions, presentations, or reading group settings. Each student should color a face to rate how he felt he did in every skill area during the discussion. Have the student record his strengths and a goal for next time at the bottom of the page.

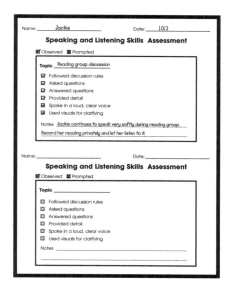

Use this page to assess and offer feedback to students after a presentation or discussion. Note the date and the topic of discussion or presentation. Use the scoring marks at the top of the page to assess each student's skills in speaking and listening. Record any observations or concerns in the *Notes* section. This page can also be used as a pretest and posttest speaking assessment.

Speaking and Listening Skills Class Proficiency

Student Name	Follows discussion rules/takes turn speaking	Asks and answers questions for understanding	Provides descriptive details	Uses drawings or other visuals to clarify	Speaks clearly and loudly

Name: _____   Date: _____

Speaking and Listening Skills

Topic _____

How did I do?

 I planned a beginning, middle, and end.

 I used pictures or props.

 I looked at my audience.

 I spoke in a loud, clear voice.

 I answered questions from the audience.

 One thing I did well _____

_____

 One thing I will work on _____

_____

Name: _____ Date: _____

Speaking and Listening Skills Assessment

☑ Observed ☒ Prompted

Topic _____

- ☐ Followed discussion rules
- ☐ Asked questions
- ☐ Answered questions
- ☐ Provided detail
- ☐ Spoke in a loud, clear voice
- ☐ Used visuals for clarifying

Notes _____

_____

Name: _____ Date: _____

Speaking and Listening Skills Assessment

☑ Observed ☒ Prompted

Topic _____

- ☐ Followed discussion rules
- ☐ Asked questions
- ☐ Answered questions
- ☐ Provided detail
- ☐ Spoke in a loud, clear voice
- ☐ Used visuals for clarifying

Notes _____

_____

Language
Standards Crosswalk

Prekindergarten*

Children should demonstrate increasing competency in the following:
- Use oral language in everyday activities.
- Print some upper- and lowercase letters.
- Speak in complete sentences.
- Understand and use a growing vocabulary.
- Understand sentences with past, future, and present verb tenses.
- Understand concepts by sorting common objects into categories.
- Apply words learned in classroom activities to real-world examples.
- Use words and phrases acquired through conversation, listening to books read aloud, activities, and play.

First Grade

Conventions of Standard English
- Use conventions of standard English grammar and usage in writing or speaking.
- Print all upper- and lowercase letters.
- Use common, proper, and possessive nouns; use singular and plural nouns with subject-verb agreement; use personal, possessive, and indefinite pronouns; use verbs to convey a sense of past, present, and future; use frequently occurring adjectives, conjunctions, and prepositions; use determiners such as *a, the, that.*
- Write and expand complete simple and compound declarative, interrogative, imperative, and exclamatory sentences in response to prompts.
- Use correct capitalization, punctuation, and spelling when writing.
- Capitalize dates and names of people; use end punctuation for sentences; use commas in dates and to separate words in a series.
- Spell words with common spelling patterns and common irregular words; spell unfamiliar words phonetically.

Knowledge of Language (Begins in Grade 2)

Vocabulary Acquisition and Use
- Use sentence-level context clues to determine the meaning of a word or phrase.
- Use frequently occurring affixes as a clue to the meaning of a word.
- Identify common root words and their inflectional forms.
- Understand word relationships and nuances in word meanings.
- Sort and define words by categories to demonstrate understanding of the concepts they represent.
- Identify real-life connections between words and their uses.
- Distinguish shades of meaning among verbs and adjectives.
- Use learned words and phrases, including common conjunctions such as *because.*

*Although Common Core State Standards are not yet available for prekindergarten, Pre-K students may be expected to demonstrate some level of competency for these skills.

Name: _____   Date: _____

Language Concepts Checklist

	Concept	Dates Taught				

Printing Uppercase and Lowercase Letters

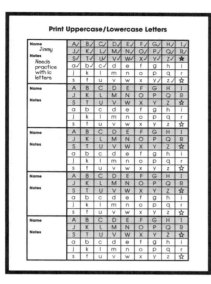

Use this page to individually assess each student's ability to print uppercase and lowercase letters and to see your class's progress at a glance. Record the names of your students in the left-hand column. For each assessment, place a check mark over or beside each letter the student can write correctly. When all of the letters have been checked off, allow the student to color the star at the end of the last row.

This page allows each student to see his progress in writing each letter. Allow the student to write each letter he masters on the blank line provided. When the student has successfully written each uppercase and lowercase letter, have him write the date at the bottom of the page. This page can also be used at home for families to keep track of the student's progress in printing uppercase and lowercase letters.

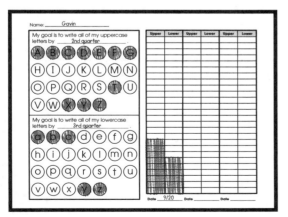

Use this page to help students track their progress in printing uppercase and lowercase letters. The student should first set a goal for being able to print all of the uppercase and lowercase letters. Each time the student is assessed, he should color in the bubbles for the letters that he has printed correctly. Then, he can date and graph the number of letters he successfully wrote for that assessment on the bar graph.

Printing Uppercase and Lowercase Letters

Name	A	B	C	D	E	F	G	H	I
	J	K	L	M	N	O	P	Q	R
Notes	S	T	U	V	W	X	Y	Z	☆
	a	b	c	d	e	f	g	h	i
	j	k	l	m	n	o	p	q	r
	s	t	u	v	w	x	y	z	☆
Name	A	B	C	D	E	F	G	H	I
	J	K	L	M	N	O	P	Q	R
Notes	S	T	U	V	W	X	Y	Z	☆
	a	b	c	d	e	f	g	h	i
	j	k	l	m	n	o	p	q	r
	s	t	u	v	w	x	y	z	☆
Name	A	B	C	D	E	F	G	H	I
	J	K	L	M	N	O	P	Q	R
Notes	S	T	U	V	W	X	Y	Z	☆
	a	b	c	d	e	f	g	h	i
	j	k	l	m	n	o	p	q	r
	s	t	u	v	w	x	y	z	☆
Name	A	B	C	D	E	F	G	H	I
	J	K	L	M	N	O	P	Q	R
Notes	S	T	U	V	W	X	Y	Z	☆
	a	b	c	d	e	f	g	h	i
	j	k	l	m	n	o	p	q	r
	s	t	u	v	w	x	y	z	☆
Name	A	B	C	D	E	F	G	H	I
	J	K	L	M	N	O	P	Q	R
Notes	S	T	U	V	W	X	Y	Z	☆
	a	b	c	d	e	f	g	h	i
	j	k	l	m	n	o	p	q	r
	s	t	u	v	w	x	y	z	☆

Name: _____

I Can Write My Letters!

A___ a___	J___ j___	S___ s___
B___ b___	K___ k___	T___ t___
C___ c___	L___ l___	U___ u___
D___ d___	M___ m___	V___ v___
E___ e___	N___ n___	W___ w___
F___ f___	O___ o___	X___ x___
G___ g___	P___ p___	Y___ y___
H___ h___	Q___ q___	Z___ z___
I___ i___	R___ r___	

Name: _____

Upper	Lower		Upper	Lower		Upper	Lower

Date _____ Date _____ Date _____

My goal is to write all of my uppercase letters by _____

(A) (B) (C) (D) (E) (F) (G)
(H) (I) (J) (K) (L) (M) (N)
(O) (P) (Q) (R) (S) (T) (U)
(V) (W) (X) (Y) (Z)

My goal is to write all of my lowercase letters by _____

(a) (b) (c) (d) (e) (f) (g)
(h) (i) (j) (k) (l) (m) (n)
(o) (p) (q) (r) (s) (t) (u)
(v) (w) (x) (y) (z)

Nouns, Plural Nouns, and Verbs

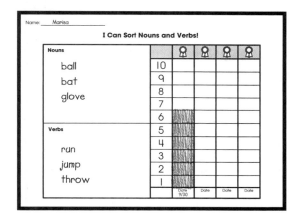

Use this page to track your class's proficiency levels in recognizing nouns, plural nouns, and verbs. Record student names in the left-hand column. Enter a level of mastery in the following columns. As you present the skills, record the date and mark *E*, *P*, or *M* (note the rating scale at the top of the page) to indicate progress of each skill. This will allow you to see at a glance which students have mastered these skills and which need help. Use the *Notes* column to write any observations or concerns.

This page gives students the opportunity to show what they know about nouns and verbs as well as track their own progress. Present five picture cards of objects (nouns) and five picture cards of a person or people performing an action (verbs) or orally call out five nouns and five verbs. Have the student place each picture card (or write the word) in the corresponding box. After each assessment, the student should write the date and color the bar graph to match the number of words that he correctly sorted.

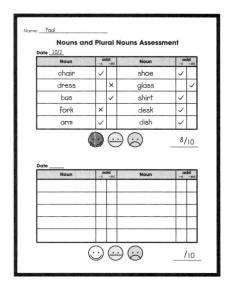

This page is useful for individual or small-group assessments in understanding plural nouns. Program the page with various nouns. Read the nouns aloud and have each student make the nouns plural by orally adding *-s* or *-es*. At the end of the assessment, have the student color a face at the bottom of the chart to show how she felt about the activity. Then, record the student's score. This assessment can be used as a pretest and posttest if desired.

Nouns and Plural Nouns Class Proficiency

E = Emerging   P = Progressing   M = Mastered

Student Name	Nouns Can identify and use	Plural Nouns Can form regular plural nouns orally by adding -s/-es	Plural Nouns Can identify and use	Notes
	☐E ☐P ☐M	☐E ☐P ☐M	☐E ☐P ☐M	
	☐E ☐P ☐M	☐E ☐P ☐M	☐E ☐P ☐M	
	☐E ☐P ☐M	☐E ☐P ☐M	☐E ☐P ☐M	
	☐E ☐P ☐M	☐E ☐P ☐M	☐E ☐P ☐M	
	☐E ☐P ☐M	☐E ☐P ☐M	☐E ☐P ☐M	
	☐E ☐P ☐M	☐E ☐P ☐M	☐E ☐P ☐M	

Name: _____

I Can Sort Nouns and Verbs!

	🎖										Date
	🎖										Date
	🎖										Date
	🎖										Date
	10	9	8	7	6	5	4	3	2	1	

Nouns

Verbs

Name: _____

Nouns and Plural Nouns Assessment

Date _____

Noun	add -s	-es	Noun	add -s	-es

            /10

Date _____

Noun	add -s	-es	Noun	add -s	-es

            /10

Prepositions

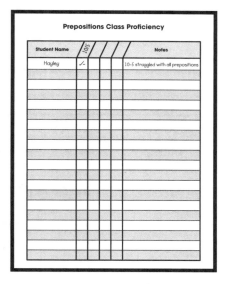

This page is useful for recording your class's proficiency in using frequently occurring prepositions (such as *to, from, in, out, on,* and *off*). Record the preposition or other identifying information, such as test date, across the top. Use a check mark system or a rating scale of your choice to record individual student proficiency in using prepositions.

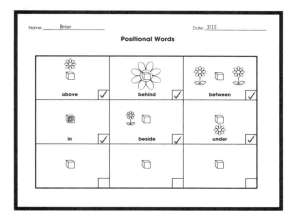

Use this page to assess each student's knowledge of positional words. The student should draw an object that demonstrates the relative position of the cube to the object she has drawn. A box is provided in each square to record a scoring mark. If desired, there is also space to introduce three additional positional words. At a later date, repeat the assessment. Keep the assessments in students' language arts portfolios to show progression in the skill of using positional words.

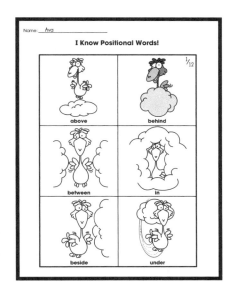

This page allows students to take ownership of learning positional words. Have each student record the date and color a bird when he has mastered the corresponding positional word. This page can also be used for parent-teacher conferences to show progress in this skill.

Prepositions Class Proficiency

Student Name					Notes

Name: _____

Date: _____

Positional Words

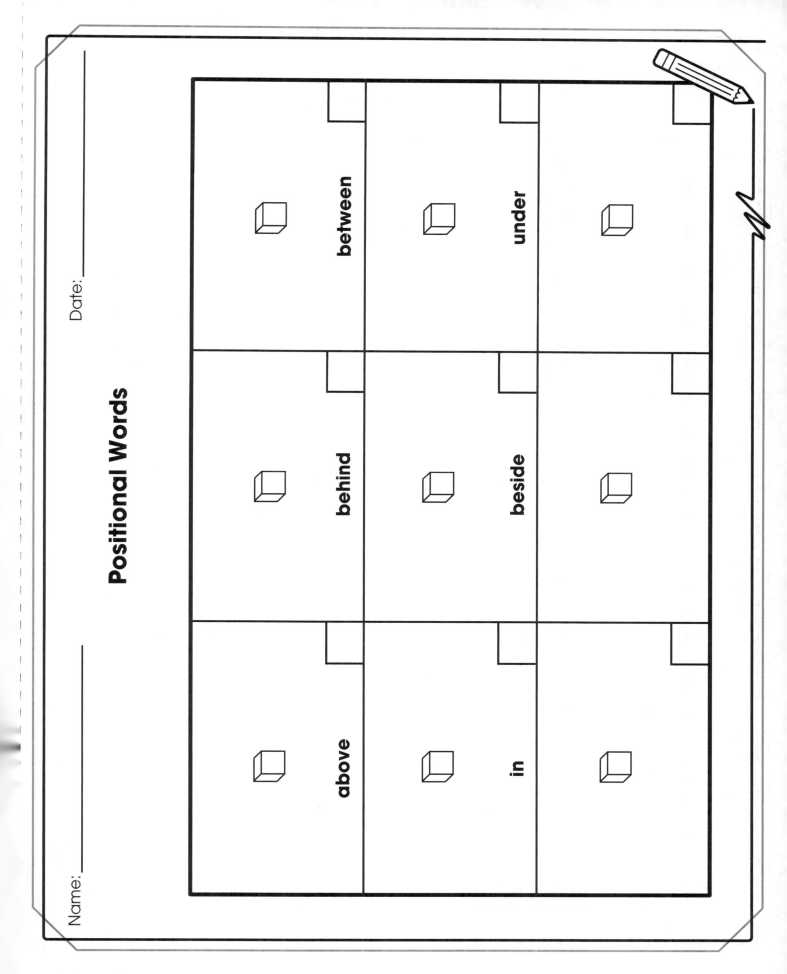

above

in

behind

beside

between

under

Name: _____

I Know Positional Words!

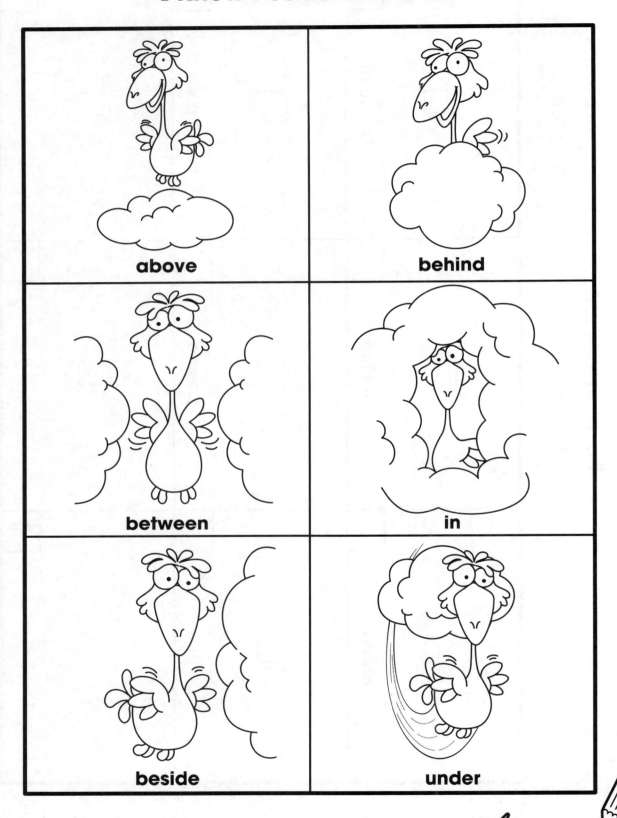

above

behind

between

in

beside

under

Sentence Structure

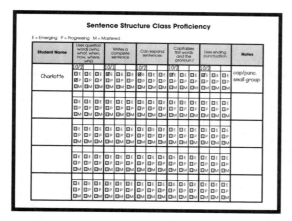

Use this page to track your class's proficiency levels as they learn correct sentence structure. Record student names in the left-hand column. Enter a level of mastery in the following columns. As you present the skills, record the date and mark *E, P,* or *M* (note the rating scale at the top of the page) to indicate the progress for each skill. This will allow you to see at a glance which students have mastered these skills and which need help. Use this page as a reference tool for principal-teacher or grade-level meetings.

This page is the perfect tool for conferencing with the student about her ability to write a complete sentence and then to expand it. Have the student write a complete sentence. She should color a face to rate herself on how she felt she did. Then, provide her with a goal for next time based on her self-assessment. After you provide further instruction on expanding sentences, the student should expand the same sentence and rate herself by coloring a face.

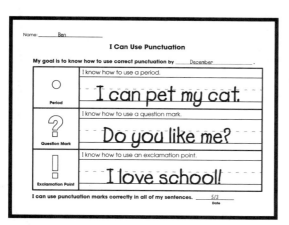

This page can be used to show proof of mastery in the skill of using correct punctuation as well as providing the student with a way to show pride in his progress. The student should first set a goal for when he wants to know how to use correct punctuation. As the student masters writing sentences with correct punctuation, allow him to demonstrate this by writing a sentence correctly in the corresponding section. Finally, have the student write the date for when he has mastered the skill of using correct punctuation.

Sentence Structure Class Proficiency

E = Emerging   P = Progressing   M = Mastered

Student Name	Uses question words (who, what, when, how, where, why)	Writes a complete sentence	Can expand sentences	Capitalizes first words and the pronoun I	Uses ending punctuation	Notes
	☐E ☐P ☐M	☐E ☐P ☐M	☐E ☐P ☐M	☐E ☐P ☐M	☐E ☐P ☐M	
	☐E ☐P ☐M	☐E ☐P ☐M	☐E ☐P ☐M	☐E ☐P ☐M	☐E ☐P ☐M	
	☐E ☐P ☐M	☐E ☐P ☐M	☐E ☐P ☐M	☐E ☐P ☐M	☐E ☐P ☐M	
	☐E ☐P ☐M	☐E ☐P ☐M	☐E ☐P ☐M	☐E ☐P ☐M	☐E ☐P ☐M	
	☐E ☐P ☐M	☐E ☐P ☐M	☐E ☐P ☐M	☐E ☐P ☐M	☐E ☐P ☐M	

Name: _____

Sentence Structure Conference

Complete Sentence   **Date** _____

- -
- -
- -

I used a capital letter	🙂 🙁	Next time I will remember to:
I wrote a complete sentence	🙂 🙁	_____
I used ending punctuation	🙂 🙁	_____

Expanded Sentence   **Date** _____

- -
- -
- -
- -
I can expand my sentence. 🙂 🙁

Name: _____

I Can Use Punctuation

My goal is to know how to use correct punctuation by _____ .

◯ **Period**	I know how to use a period.
❓ ▢ **Question Mark**	I know how to use a question mark.
▭ ▢ **Exclamation Point**	I know how to use an exclamation point.

I can use punctuation marks correctly in all of my sentences. _____
Date

Language Skills

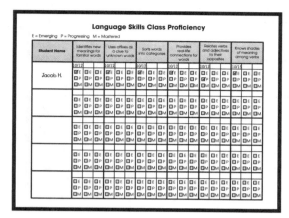

Use this page to track your class's proficiency levels in various language skills. Record student names in the left-hand column. Enter a level of mastery in the following columns. As you present the skills, record the date and mark *E*, *P*, or *M* (note the rating scale at the top of the page) to indicate the progress for each skill. This will allow you to see at a glance which students have mastered these skills and which need help. Use this page as a reference tool for principal-teacher or grade-level meetings.

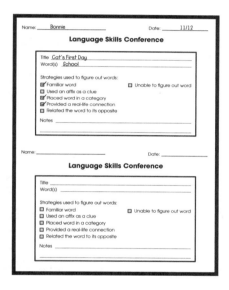

This page is ideal for conferencing and gaining insight into how a student is using his strategies to figure out new words. It can be used individually or in reading groups. Write the title of the book and present a passage to the student to read. Choose a word that the student seems to struggle with while reading. Record the word and which strategies he used to figure out the word. Record any observations or concerns in the *Notes* section. This assessment can be used as a pretest and posttest if desired.

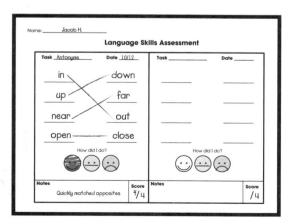

This page can be used for assessing various skills in language arts. Record the task and date at the top of the assessment. Choose four pairs of words that relate to each other, such as synonyms, adjectives, word parts (affixes), etc. Have the student draw a line to match the word pairs correctly. The student should color a face to show how she felt she did on the activity. Then, record the student's score. Write any observations or concerns in the *Notes* section.

Language Skills Class Proficiency

E = Emerging   P = Progressing   M = Mastered

Student Name	Identifies new meanings for familiar words			Uses affixes as a clue to unknown words			Sorts words into categories			Provides real-life connections for words			Relates verbs and adjectives to their opposites			Knows shades of meaning among verbs		
	☐E ☐P ☐M	☐E ☐P ☐M	☐E ☐P ☐M	☐E ☐P ☐M	☐E ☐P ☐M	☐E ☐P ☐M	☐E ☐P ☐M	☐E ☐P ☐M	☐E ☐P ☐M	☐E ☐P ☐M	☐E ☐P ☐M	☐E ☐P ☐M	☐E ☐P ☐M	☐E ☐P ☐M	☐E ☐P ☐M	☐E ☐P ☐M	☐E ☐P ☐M	☐E ☐P ☐M
	☐E ☐P ☐M	☐E ☐P ☐M	☐E ☐P ☐M	☐E ☐P ☐M	☐E ☐P ☐M	☐E ☐P ☐M	☐E ☐P ☐M	☐E ☐P ☐M	☐E ☐P ☐M	☐E ☐P ☐M	☐E ☐P ☐M	☐E ☐P ☐M	☐E ☐P ☐M	☐E ☐P ☐M	☐E ☐P ☐M	☐E ☐P ☐M	☐E ☐P ☐M	☐E ☐P ☐M
	☐E ☐P ☐M	☐E ☐P ☐M	☐E ☐P ☐M	☐E ☐P ☐M	☐E ☐P ☐M	☐E ☐P ☐M	☐E ☐P ☐M	☐E ☐P ☐M	☐E ☐P ☐M	☐E ☐P ☐M	☐E ☐P ☐M	☐E ☐P ☐M	☐E ☐P ☐M	☐E ☐P ☐M	☐E ☐P ☐M	☐E ☐P ☐M	☐E ☐P ☐M	☐E ☐P ☐M
	☐E ☐P ☐M	☐E ☐P ☐M	☐E ☐P ☐M	☐E ☐P ☐M	☐E ☐P ☐M	☐E ☐P ☐M	☐E ☐P ☐M	☐E ☐P ☐M	☐E ☐P ☐M	☐E ☐P ☐M	☐E ☐P ☐M	☐E ☐P ☐M	☐E ☐P ☐M	☐E ☐P ☐M	☐E ☐P ☐M	☐E ☐P ☐M	☐E ☐P ☐M	☐E ☐P ☐M
	☐E ☐P ☐M	☐E ☐P ☐M	☐E ☐P ☐M	☐E ☐P ☐M	☐E ☐P ☐M	☐E ☐P ☐M	☐E ☐P ☐M	☐E ☐P ☐M	☐E ☐P ☐M	☐E ☐P ☐M	☐E ☐P ☐M	☐E ☐P ☐M	☐E ☐P ☐M	☐E ☐P ☐M	☐E ☐P ☐M	☐E ☐P ☐M	☐E ☐P ☐M	☐E ☐P ☐M